ANSWER KEY

Classical Subjects *Creatively* Taught™

French for Children

Primer B

Learn more than how to order a croissant

Joshua Kraut, PhD
with David Spieser, PhD

French for Children Primer B Answer Key

Version 1.0

ISBN: 978-1-60051-297-1

Classical Academic Press
515 S. 32nd Street
Camp Hill, PA 17011

www.ClassicalAcademicPress.com

Illustrations by Jason Rayner
Book design by Lenora Riley

PGP.02.21

TABLE OF CONTENTS

TEACHER'S NOTE

Please note that this table of contents pertains to the student edition and is supplied for your ease of use when directing students to specific sections of the book. This answer key does not contain the Memory or Grammar pages from the student edition and therefore much of the pagination will be different than that of the student edition.

*These sections are continued from *FFCA*. See page 5 for a note about this.

CD Track & Audio File Information

CD Track	Audio File	Chap.	Page
1	01_01	1	9
2	01_02	1	10
3	01_03	1	10
4	01_04	1	11
5	01_05	1	11
6	01_06	1	15
7	01_07	1	20
8	02_01	2	21
9	02_02	2	22
10	02_03	2	22
11	02_04	2	22
12	02_05	2	27
13	02_06	2	32
14	03_01	3	33
15	03_02	3	34
16	03_03	3	34
17	03_04	3	34
18	03_05	3	38
19	03_06	3	44
20	04_01	4	45
21	04_02	4	46
22	04_03	4	46
23	04_04	4	46
24	04_05	4	47/51
25	04_06	4	56
26	05_01	5	60
27	06_01	6	65
28	06_02	6	66
29	06_03	6	66
30	06_04	6	66
31	06_05	6	71
32	06_06	6	74
33	07_01	7	75
34	07_02	7	76
35	07_03	7	76
36	07_04	7	76
37	07_05	7	80
38	07_06	7	84
39	08_01	8	85
40	08_02	8	86
41	08_03	8	86
42	08_04	8	86
43	08_05	8	91
44	08_06	8	96
45	09_01	9	97
46	09_02	9	98
47	09_03	9	98
48	09_04	9	98
49	09_05	9	100
50	09_06	9	101
51	09_07	9	101
52	09_08	9	101
53	09_09	9	102
54	09_10	9	108
55	10_01	10	118
56	11_01	11	119
57	11_02	11	120
58	11_03	11	120
59	11_04	11	120
60	11_05	11	125
61	11_06	11	130
62	12_01	12	131
63	12_02	12	132
64	12_03	12	133
65	12_04	12	133
66	12_05	12	133
67	12_06	12	142
68	12_07	12	144
69	13_01	13	145
70	13_02	13	146
71	13_03	13	146
72	13_04	13	146
73	13_05	13	150
74	13_06	13	155
75	13_07	13	156
76	14_01	14	157
77	14_02	14	158
78	14_03	14	158
79	14_04	14	158
80	14_05	14	165
81	14_06	14	170
82	15_01	15	171
83	15_02	15	172
84	15_03	15	172
85	15_04	15	172
86	15_05	15	184
87	15_06	15	186

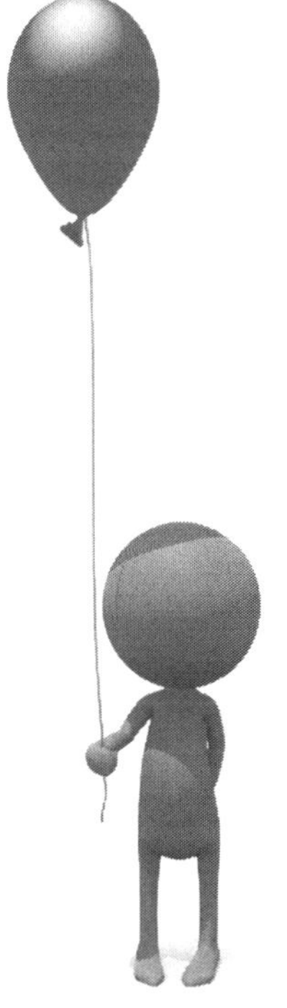

Suggested Schedule

There are seventeen chapters in *French for Children Primer B*, thirteen of which are content chapters and four are review. Doing one chapter per week (content and review chapters) will allow you to finish the course in approximately half of an academic year. Alternatively, if you complete one content chapter every two weeks, taking just one week per review chapter, the course will take a full year—thirty weeks.

Weekly Schedule

The following is a basic weekly schedule, to be modified as necessary by the teacher. Note that days two and five call for longer sessions.

Day One (approx. 30 mins.)

Listen to the audio file of the opening dialogue and have students follow along in the text. Take a few minutes (not too long) to ask students what they've understood from the dialogue and what they think is going on. Total comprehension at this stage is not essential; students should be encouraged to guess at the details of the plot or simply the meaning of new vocabulary items based on context. Present the vocabulary and the paradigm (grammar chant). Students should chant through the paradigm and vocabulary two or three times, using the recorded audio files (and/or teachers' pronunciation) as a guide. (Optional step 1: At this point, the video can be played up to the point at which the instructor reads through the chant and the vocabulary, but the video should be stopped after that.) Then, ask students to skim back over the dialogue to see if they understand more of the French. Again, do not take too long for comprehension questions at this stage; the dialogue will be revisited later. (Optional step 2: Students can take turns reading different parts in the dialogue, one or two lines each. This activity is meant to help students read the French and develop good French pronunciation more than to stage a drama, since students may not understand every word of the dialogue.)

Day Two (approx. 55–65 mins.)

Review the paradigm (grammar chant) and vocabulary and have students chant them again one or two times. Watch the video (either picking up where you left off from day one or viewing it in its entirety). The videos are approximately forty-five minutes to an hour in length. While you should feel free to stop them and rewind at any time, be aware that they may take a while to get through with frequent interruptions.

Day Three (approx. 30 mins.)

Start with a quick chant of the paradigm and vocabulary. Then spend some time explaining the grammar page, paying special attention to the examples. If you see an italicized sentence, be sure to emphasize it (you may consider having students circle these and other key sentences with a colored pencil for future reference). Ask comprehension questions, such as "What two words do you need to turn a positive sentence into a negative one in French?" or "What is an irregular verb?" After this, begin the worksheet, or assign it as homework.

Day Four (approx. 30 mins.)

Again, start the day with a quick chant of the paradigm and vocabulary. Next, the worksheet should either be started or completed. Check students' work and go over any corrections with the students. Grammar should be reviewed and retaught as necessary. One means of reviewing grammar can be to view the video again to ensure comprehension of key grammatical topics for that chapter.

Day Five (approx. 50 mins.)

Students should take the quiz without looking back at the rest of the chapter. When the quiz has been completed, go over the answers together and review any trouble spots. Finally, go back and listen to the opening dialogue once more, having students follow along in the text. Discuss what is happening, and identify vocabulary/grammatical points that help in understanding the dialogue. Translate the dialogue together.

Biweekly Schedule

The following is a basic biweekly schedule spread over seven class meetings, to be modified as necessary by the teacher.

Day One (approx. 30 mins.)

Listen to the opening dialogue and follow along in the text. Take a few minutes (not too long) to ask students what they've understood from the dialogue, and what they think is going on. Total comprehension at this stage is not essential; students should be encouraged to guess at the details of the plot or simply the meaning of new vocabulary items based on context. Present the vocabulary and the paradigm (grammar chant). Students should chant through the paradigm and vocabulary two or three times, using the recorded audio files (and/or teachers' pronunciation) as a guide. (Optional step 1: At this point, the video can be played up to the point at which the instructor reads through the chant and the vocabulary, but it should be stopped after that.) Then, ask students to skim back over the dialogue to see if they understand more of the French. Again, do not take too long for comprehension questions at this stage; the dialogue will be revisited later. (Optional step 2: Students can take turns reading different parts in the dialogue, one or two lines each. This activity is meant to help students read and develop good French pronunciation more than to stage a drama, since students may not understand every word of the dialogue.)

Day Two (approx. 55–65 mins.)

Review the paradigm (grammar chant) and vocabulary and have students chant them again one or two times. Have students watch the video (either picking up where you left off from day one, or else in its entirety). The videos are between forty-five minutes and an hour in length. While you should feel free to stop them and rewind at any time, be aware that they may take a while to get through with frequent interruptions.

Day Three (approx. 30 mins.)

Start with a quick chant of the paradigm and vocabulary. Then spend some time explaining the grammar page, paying special attention to the examples. If you see an italicized sentence, be sure to emphasize it (you may consider having students circle or highlight these and other key sentences for future reference). Ask comprehension questions, such as "What two words do you need to turn a positive sentence into a negative one in French?" or "What is an irregular verb?" Go back and listen to the opening dialogue once more, having students follow along in the text. Discuss what is happening, and identify vocabulary/grammatical points that help in the understanding of the dialogue (a full translation is not necessary at this time—target in particular those sections of the dialogue that employ grammatical notions discussed in the Grammar section). If time remains, have students begin the worksheet.

Day Four (approx. 30 mins.)

Again, start the day with a quick chant of the paradigm and vocabulary. Next, the worksheet should be started. Students may consult the chapter to complete this section. Grammar should be reviewed and retaught as necessary. One means of reviewing grammar can be to view parts of the video again to ensure comprehension of key grammatical topics for that chapter.

Day Five (approx. 30 mins.)

The worksheet should be completed and reviewed. Trouble spots should be addressed. Students should prepare for taking the quiz by playing vocabulary games (e.g., flash cards, bingo, charades, etc.).

Day Six (approx. 30 mins.)

Have students take the quiz, noting that they are not to look back at the previous sections of the chapter.

Day Seven (approx. 30 mins.)

Review the quiz. Then, return a final time to the opening dialogue, having students listen to the audio file and follow along in the text. Translate the dialogue together. Discuss what is happening and identify vocabulary/grammatical points that help you understand the dialogue. Students may be encouraged to read aloud and to do their best to "act the part" if they feel so inclined.

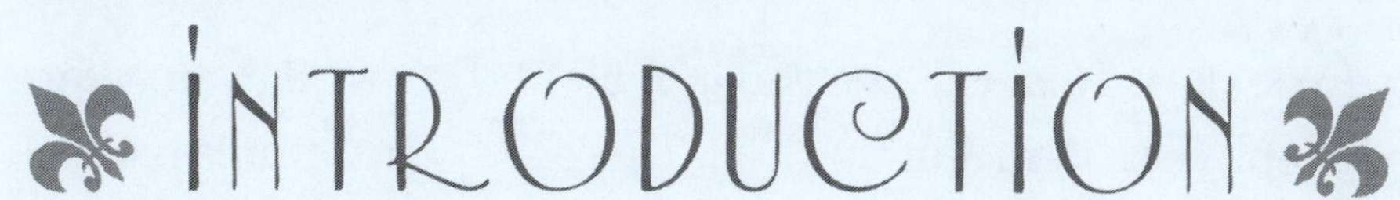

Introduction

Welcome back for another exciting course in French! *French for Children Primer B* (*FFCB*) picks up right where the previous volume—*French for Children Primer A* (*FFCA*)—left off. In fact, if you look at the table of contents in this book, you'll see that some of the "series" of grammatical themes simply continue on here. For example, we're beginning in chapter 1 with part 2 in our discussion of irregular verbs—that's a continuation of part 1 from *FFCA*. You'll come across other grammatical units that began in *FFCA* and are expanded upon in this book, so if you see a part 3 of some unit that appears to be missing the first two parts, make sure you have a look back at *FFCA*!

Just as a reminder, then, there are two types of chapters in this book: *lesson chapters* and *review chapters*. Review chapters bring together the information you've seen in the previous few chapters, and give you an opportunity to test your knowledge. Lesson chapters are where you learn things for the first time.

In each lesson chapter, you will see a few things: At the top of each page in the lesson chapters, you will see different titles. The title that is BIGGER THAN THE REST tells you which part of a chapter you are in. The four main parts of each lesson chapter are: Memory, Grammar, Worksheet, or Quiz. Let's take a look at what you'll find in each of the different parts.

Memory

Dialogue

The dialogues in this book continue to tell the tale of Jean and Aurélie, whom you met in *FFCA*. As in that book, the dialogues in this book introduce you to some of the new vocabulary that you'll be learning in each lesson chapter. Feel free to read over the chapter's vocabulary list before reading the dialogue if you desire, but we do not recommend that you try to memorize the vocabulary letter-for-letter before attempting to read the dialogues.

The most rewarding way to approach the dialogues may simply be to *jump right in and try to figure out what words mean by their context.* The mix of French and English within the dialogues continues in this book, though with more emphasis on the French. As with *FFCA*, this mixture of languages should make it possible for you to decipher the new French words in each chapter. Even if you can only narrow it down to a guess (for example: "I think this word must be some kind of food," or "I think this word is an action that means to go somewhere"), that's a great start. This will give you a "feel" for the word even before you study the vocabulary more deeply (see item 3 in this list). There are translations of all of the dialogues in the back of the teacher's edition of *FFCB* (see Appendix A: Dialogue Translations).

Chant

The French word **chant** means the same thing as the English word "chant," so you already know what this is! In each chapter we ask you to chant a certain set of words or phrases. Why? The goal is to help you and your mouth get used to forming the sounds of these words. You can listen to the audio files of the chants. The chants and their translations are also included in their own appendix (appendix B) at the end of this book.

Vocabulaire

There are approximately ten vocabulary words in each chapter. After reading through the dialogue and trying to figure out the new words ahead of time, we recommend that you spend a few minutes committing these words to memory every day that you are working on the chapter. Memorize the vocabulary, and following the chapter will be easy as pie. Don't memorize it, and you'll be flipping pages back and forth the whole time to look up what the words mean! As a way of making memorizing the vocabulary easier, try creating flash cards and having someone quiz you with them.

Grammar

This section is where we discuss the inner workings of French grammar—and how to use it. Pay close attention to a few different *icons* that may appear on the pages of the Grammar section:

***Remarque*:** The French word **remarque** looks like an English word you may know—"remark." In this book, when you see the **Remarque** icon, this means that you will be given a little bit of extra information to remember about the grammar rule you've just learned.

***Renvoi*:** A **renvoi** is a sort of reminder to go back to a subject that has already been mentioned. For example, if we are talking about something in chapter 7, which uses some of the information from chapter 2, there will be a **Renvoi** icon in chapter 7, which tells you "Turn to chapter 2 if you need to refresh your memory."

Worksheet

The Worksheet is just what the name says it is: worksheet exercises where you can put your brain to the test and see if you can use the grammar lesson to complete the charts, sentences, and word puzzles you'll find. For the Worksheet, feel free to flip back and forth between the exercises and the pages in the Grammar section in case you get stuck; the idea is to learn as you go. Answers to the exercises from both the Worksheet and the Quiz sections are found in *French for Children Primer B Answer Key*.

An additional note on the answer key: In *FFCA*, for present-tense verb phrases, such as **je parle**, we supplied two translations: "I speak/I am speaking." Both translations were included in the answer key. In *FFCB*, we will no longer provide both translations since we'll be introducing even more expressions that could be translated multiple ways. It would be too complicated, for instance, to list four different possible translations for a sentence that combined a present-tense verb and another one of these expressions! However, specifically on the topic of the verb translations, you can rest assured that both translations are still appropriate unless it is clearly a situation in which one seems more natural than the other. The key is simply to know in the back of your mind when you'd use one translation and when you'd use the other.

Quiz

Finally, the end of each lesson chapter contains a Quiz section. This section is similar to the Worksheet, except this time you're *only* supposed to use your brain—no looking back at the Grammar section, the Worksheet, your flash cards, your notes, nothing, zero, zip, **rien** (**rien** is French for "nothing"). Of course, **la police** won't come to your house if you do go back and look, but the point is that *if you still need to go back to previous pages for help, you have not really learned the lesson*, and so you should probably not go on to the next chapter until you can pass the quiz with either a perfect score or only one or two answers wrong. And, of course, once you're done with the quiz, we highly recommend going back to the opening dialogue and reading it through once more—probably much faster, and more enjoyably this time!—to cement in all of the new things you've learned.

La dictée

At the end of every Quiz section we've included an exercise called a **dictée**—a dictation exercise. Traditionally in this exercise, the teacher reads a short sentence slowly, a few words at a time, and the students copy down, or transcribe, what they hear. You can hear the sentences read on the CD or audio file. (Check the CD Track & Audio File Information page for the list of the **dictée** associated with each chapter.) If the teacher feels comfortable doing so, he or she may read the sentences aloud as well, including perhaps a faster repetition (one which approaches a normal speech rate) the second time.

Transcribing spoken French is especially helpful since, as you'll see, there are many letters that you may not hear pronounced, but which are important to include in the written form nonetheless. In fact, the **dictée** has a rich tradition in francophone culture, believe it or not—a bit like our spelling bees. Today in the francophone world there are **dictée** competitions in many different regions, and they attract both schoolchildren and adults! Our hope is that these "spoken puzzles" will be challenging and instructive for you as well.

Here are a few practical tips regarding **dictées**:

First, you should feel free to incorporate the **dictées** in the Worksheet section if you find that more helpful, or if it works more neatly with your schedule. Second, as for the marking of the **dictées** (assuming they are being used in a Quiz), the instructor should be generous with "partial credit" in these exercises. It can be quite challenging to get the entire sentence exactly right, so having a breakdown of how students can obtain points for each sentence—rather using an all-or-nothing scheme—would be preferable. One could award points, for example, for each correctly spelled word.

Treasures in the Back of the Book: New Material in *FFCB*

Far, far away, in the back of this book, you will find several things:

Appendices

The appendices contain some of the same information you will learn from the book's regular lesson chapters, but it is condensed and organized into charts in the appendices to make it easier to search through. There is a preposition appendix (appendix E; prepositions appear throughout this book), verb appendix (appendix C) with verb conjugations, and a past participle appendix (appendix D; also see chapter 11).

Glossaries

The alphabetical glossary contains all of the vocabulary items in this book, along with their translations, presented in one long, alphabetical list. Think of this section as a "mini-dictionary" that contains the words for both *FFCA* and *FFCB*. For nouns, you will see the clues to determining the noun's gender in the glossary entry. In the glossary by chapter—you guessed it—all of the vocabulary words from *FFCB* are listed by the chapter in which they first appear. This glossary can be a very handy tool when you're studying your vocabulary. You will also find a categorical glossary that divides the book's vocabulary, along with the Conversation Journal words and phrases, into various categories based on how they are used

Traduction

Of course, during Jean and Aurélie's absence from the zoo, their keepers have been searching all over for their escaped animals. Here are the two missing-animal posters that have been put up around town to help track them down. Translate Jean's poster from French to English; then translate Aurélie's poster from English to French!

Avis de Recherche!*

Il s'appelle Jean.
Il est une souris.
Il a onze ans.
Ses yeux sont bleus.
Son nez est rouge.
Ses oreilles sont petites.
Il est très intelligent et sympa.

Avis de Recherche!

Her name is Aurélie.
She is a cow.
She is eleven years old.
She is very funny.
Her eyes are green.
She has four big legs.
Her mouth is very big.

His name is Jean.
He is a mouse.
He is eleven years old.
His eyes are blue.
His nose is red.
His ears are small.
He is very intelligent and nice.

Elle s'appelle Aurélie.
Elle est une vache.
Elle a onze ans.
Elle est très amusante.
Ses yeux sont verts.
Elle a quatre grandes jambes.
Sa bouche est très grande.

*Missing Person Notice

Say It Aloud!

The following are sentences that (we could imagine) come from Jean and Aurélie's meeting with Thibault. Fill in the blanks using the different conjugations you've learned for the verb **être**. Then, translate the sentences. Finally, say them out loud and compare your pronunciation to what you hear on the audio file [01_06/Tr. 6].

1. **Jean et Aurélie habitent dans le zoo. Le zoo** ___est___ **dans la ville.**

   Translation: Jean and Aurélie live in the zoo. The zoo is in the city.

2. **La maison de Thibault** ___est___ **dans un petit village.**

   Translation: Thibault's house is in a little village.

3. **Ses sœurs** ___sont___ **jeunes. Elles ont cinq, sept, et neuf ans!**

   Translation: His sisters are young. They are five, seven, and nine years old!

4. **"Aurélie, tu** ___es___ **intelligente!"**

   Translation: "Aurelie, you are intelligent!"

5. **"Nous avons peur de voyager, alors nous** ___sommes___ **contents de marcher ensemble."**

   Translation: "We are afraid to travel, so we are happy to walk together."

6. **Thibault a envie de marcher à la ville: "Moi aussi! Je** ___suis___ **très content de marcher à la ville avec vous. Vous** ___êtes___ **très sympas."**

   Translation: Thibault wants to walk to the city: "Me too! I am very happy to walk to the city with you. You are very nice."

Grammaire

Circle the correct answer.

1. The verb **être** does not follow a normal pattern, so we call it:

   a. erratic.

   b. regular.

   c. irregular.

   d. unreliable.

2. When you say, "**Mes amis *sont* sympas,**"

   a. you cannot hear the **t** in **sont**.

   b. you cannot hear the **n** in **sont**.

   c. you cannot hear the **n** or the **t** in **sont**.

   d. you can hear all of the letters in **sont**.

3. If you saw a note lying on the ground that said, "**Merci! Je suis contente!**" the one thing you could be sure of is that:

   a. The author of the note is sad.

   b. The author of the note is a female.

   c. The author of the note is in trouble.

   d. The author of the note is mean.

4. How do you say, "I like to be at school" in French?

   a. **Il aime est à l'école.**

   b. **Je suis aimer à l'école.**

   c. **J'aime être à l'école.**

   d. **J'aime suis l'école.**

Nouveau Vocabulaire

Fill in the blank with the correct translation(s) for each word.

Français	Anglais
1. **être, je suis**	to be, I am
2. **voyager, je voyage**	to travel, I travel
3. **visiter, je visite**	to visit, I visit
4. **avoir envie de, j'ai envie de**	to feel like/to want, I feel like/I want
5. **un endroit**	a place
6. **une idée**	an idea
7. **ensemble**	together
8. **intelligent/bête**	smart/dumb
9. **content/triste**	happy/sad
10. **difficile/simple**	difficult/simple

Ancien Vocabulaire

Fill in the blank with the correct translation(s) for each word.

Français	Anglais
1. **le genou**	the knee
2. **regarder, je regarde**	to look (at), I look (at)
3. **la grange**	the barn
4. **avoir besoin de, j'ai besoin de**	to need, I need
5. **porter, je porte**	to carry, I carry
6. **mignon**	cute

Français	Anglais
7. **méchant**	mean
8. **l'eau**	the water
9. **mais**	but
10. **un enfant**	a child

Hide-and-Seek Conjugation

Somewhere in the following chart, there is a verb form from another verb that is trying to hide in this conjugation chart. It's playing hide-and-seek with you. Seek it out, circle it, and then add the correct conjugation for **être**. Make sure you write the translations for all the other conjugations, too (we've left space inside the chart so you can stick them right in there).

REMARQUE

In French, the game hide-and-seek is called **cache-cache**, which literally means "hide-hide" in English.

Person	Singular	Plural
1st Person	**je suis** ______ (I am)	**nous sommes** ______ (we are)
2nd Person	**tu es** ______ (you are)	**vous avez** êtes (you are)
3rd Person	**il/elle est** ______ (he/she/it is)	**ils/elles sont** ______ (they are)

Traduction: The Être Staircase

Translate the following sentences into French, and see if you can make it to the bottom of the staircase full of **être** verbs. Don't forget to make those adjectives agree with the subjects in gender and number!

I am happy. **Je suis content.**

You are happy. **Tu es content.**

You are sad. **Tu es triste.**

He is sad. **Il est triste.**

He is interesting. **Il est intéressant.**

She is interesting. **Elle est intéressante.**

She is intelligent. **Elle est intelligente.**

We[6] are intelligent. **Nous sommes intelligents.**

We are funny. **Nous sommes amusants.**

You[7] (**vous**) are funny. **Vous êtes amusants.**

You are handsome. **Vous êtes beaux.**

They are handsome. **Ils sont beaux.**

They are beautiful. **Elles sont belles.**

6. We don't know the gender of "we" in this sentence, so let's imagine that "we" is a mix of males and females, then.
7. Again, let's assume that this is a mix of males and females.

Dictée!

Listen to the audio file [01_07/Tr. 7] of the **dictée** for this **chapitre**. On the lines provided, write down the three sentences you hear. You do not need to write translations for them, though it's good practice to think through what the English translation would be. You may stop and repeat the audio file several times as you're writing down the sentences.

1. **Nous sommes très contents.**

   Translation: We are very happy.

2. **J'ai envie de voyager avec mes amis.**

   Translation: I feel like traveling with my friends.

3. **Les devoirs sont difficiles!**

   Translation: The homework is difficult!

TEACHER'S NOTE

Homework is a plural noun in French, though it is singular in English!

Teacher's Note

The gray text indicates translations that are not provided in the student edition. We thought it would be helpful to supply teachers with translations where applicable.

Chant

Remplir (fill in) **le tableau** (the chart/table).

Person	Singular	Plural
1st Person	**je vais** (I go)	nous allons (we go)
2nd Person	tu vas (you go)	vous allez (you go)
3rd Person	il/elle va (he/she/it goes)	ils/elles vont (they go)
—	Vas-y! (Go on! Keep going!)	Allez-y! (Go on! Keep going!)

In the following sentences, fill in the blanks with the correct forms of the verb **aller** (to go). Remember, you can use the infinitive form **aller**, too! An example is provided below.

Exemple: L'oiseau et le renard vont à la montagne.
The bird and the fox go to the mountain.

Remarque

In *FFCA*, present-tense verb phrases such as **vont à la montagne** were translated as "go to the mountain" *or* "are going to the mountain." The examples and answer key reflected both possibilities. In *FFCB*, we will no longer provide both translations since we'll be introducing even more expressions that could be translated multiple ways. It would be too complicated, for instance, to list four different possible translations for a sentence that combined a present-tense verb and another one of these expressions! However, you can rest assured that both translations are still appropriate unless it is clearly a situation in which one translation seems more natural than the other. The key is simply to know in the back of your mind when you'd use one translation and when you'd use the other.

1. **Le loup** ____va____ **aux champs.** The wolf goes to the fields.
2. **Jean et Aurélie** ____vont____ **à la ville.** Jean and Aurélie go to the city.
3. **Le meunier (the miller)** ____va____ **à la foire.** The miller goes to the fair.

4. **Le loup parle: "Tu ___va___ aux champs?"**
   The wolf is speaking: "You are going to the fields?"
5. **Le meunier parle: "Non, je ___vais___ à la foire."**
   The miller is speaking: "No, I am going to the fair."
6. **Jean et Aurélie parlent: "Nous ___allons___ à la ville."**
   Jean and Aurélie are speaking: "We are going to the city."
7. **Le loup parle à Jean et Aurélie: "Ah, vous ___allez___ à la ville! Très bien!"**
   The wolf is speaking to Jean and Aurélie: "Oh, you are going to the city! Very good!"
8. **Thibault parle à Jean et Aurélie: "J'ai envie d' ___aller___ avec vous!"**
   Thibault is speaking to Jean and Aurélie: "I want to go with you!"
9. **Finalement (finally), Thibault ___va___ à la ville avec Jean et Aurélie.**
   Finally, Thibault goes to the city with Jean and Aurelie.

Say It Aloud! The Acrobatic À

Remplir (Fill in) **les trous** (the holes) in the following sentences by circling the correct kind of Acrobatic **à**—that is: **à**, **à la**, **au**, or **aux**. (Hint: We've given you the gender of the noun—either masculine [m.] or feminine [f.]—that follows the preposition in each sentence. Sometimes you'll need it, sometimes you won't!) Once you've chosen the correct Acrobatic **à**, translate the sentences into English. Finally, go back and pronounce the complete sentence in French, comparing your pronunciation to what you hear on the audio file (02_05/Tr. 12).

1. **J'aime les endroits intéressants. J'aime aller ________ endroits (m.) intéressants.**
   [à / à la / au / (aux)]

   Translation: I like interesting places. I like to go to interesting places.

2. **Vous allez ________ zoo (m.)?**
   [à / à la / (au) / aux]

   Translation: You are going to the zoo?

3. **Je suis berger. Je vais ________ champs (m.)!**
   [à / à la / au / (aux)]

   Translation: I am a shepherd. I am going to the fields!

4. **Ma sœur est paresseuse. Elle reste ________ maison (f.).**
   [à / (à la) / au / aux]

   Translation: My sister is lazy. She stays home/she stays in the house.

5. **Tu parles _________ enfants (m.) méchants?**
   [à / à la / au / (aux)]

   Translation: Are you speaking to mean children?

6. **Mon frère va _________ une grande école (f.).**
   [(à) / à la / au / aux]

   Translation: My brother goes to a big school.

7. **Tu restes _________ maison (f.) aujourd'hui?**
   [à / (à la) / au / aux]

   Translation: Are you staying home/in the house today?

Grammaire

Circle the correct answer.

1. The words **à**, **de**, and **dans** are examples of a kind of word called a __________.

   (a.) preposition

   b. conjunction

   c. article

   d. adverb

2. If you heard just the two words **au** and **aux** read aloud one after the other, the difference in pronunciation:

   a. would be like the difference between "oh" and "oaks."

   b. would be fairly small.

   (c.) does not exist.

   d. would be similar to the difference between "aw" and "ox."

3. Which two words will you *never* see next to each other in French?

   a. **aller** and **à**

   b. **aller** and **aux**

   c. **à** and **la**

   (d.) **à** and **le**

Nouveau Vocabulaire

Fill in the blank with the correct translation(s) for each word.

Français	Anglais
1. **aller, je vais**	to go, I go
2. **un manteau**	a coat
3. **un chapeau**	a hat
4. **une chemise**	a shirt
5. **un pantalon**	pants
6. **une chaussure/chaussette**	a shoe, a sock
7. **un mouton**	a sheep
8. **un berger**	a shepherd
9. **une foire**	a fair
10. **un loup**	a wolf
11. **porter, je porte**	to wear, I wear; to carry I carry

Ancien Vocabulaire, Special Edition—Prepositions

Fill in the blank with the correct translation(s) for each word. No peeking at the list in this **chapitre**!

Français	Anglais
1. **à**	to, at
2. **à côté de**	next to
3. **avec**	with
4. **dans**	in

Français	Anglais
5. **de**	of, from
6. **loin (de)**	far (from)
7. **pour**	for
8. **près (de)**	near (to), close (to)
9. **sur**	on, on top of
10. **vers**	toward

Prepositional Family Reunion!

In the following sentences, the Daring **de** joins forces with its distant cousin, the Acrobatic **à** to form fantastic new **phrases**.[4] Isn't it handy to be able to say where people come from and where they are going to? Just as in the Worksheet section, the goal of this exercise is for you to pick the correct preposition from the choices below each blank and circle it. Check *FFCA* **chapitre** 11 if you run into trouble with the preposition **de**. Once you've chosen the correct preposition, translate the **phrases** into English.

1. **Les animaux vont ________ grange (f.) ________ forêt (f.).**
   de / (de la) / du / des — **à / (à la) / au / aux**

   Translation: The animals are going from the barn to the forest.

2. **Ma famille marche ________ village (m.) ________ montagne (f.).**
   de / de la / (du) / des — **à / (à la) / au / aux**

   Translation: My family is walking from the village to the mountain.

3. **Les oiseaux volent ________ arbres (m.) ________ champs (m.).**
   d'un / d'une / (des) — **à / à la / au / (aux)**

   Translation: The birds fly from the trees to the fields.

4. **Une phrase** means "a sentence." As you say the word in the plural, though, don't forget that we drop the final **s** on **phrases**—*FRAHZ*." When you want to say the English word "phrase" in French, you'd say **une expression**. And then, to say "an expression," such as an idiom, or something like that, you . . . Hey! What are you doing still reading this footnote!? Go back to the Quiz!

4. **Notre chien va ______________ maison (f.) ______________ école (f.) pour**
de / (de la) / du / des — **à / (à l') / au / aux**

chercher notre petite sœur.

Translation: **Our dog is going from the house to the school to look for our little sister.**

5. **Ils voyagent ______________ petit village (m.) ______________ grande ville (f).**
(d'un) / d'une / des — **à / (à la) / au / aux**

Translation: **They are traveling from a little village to the big city.**

Oú Vont-Ils? (Where Are They Going?)

Complétez les phrases (complete the sentences) **avec un sujet** (with a subject), unless there already is one (as in sentences 3 and 5), **et le verbe aller** (and the verb **aller**) in the appropriate form. You do not need to write out the full translation into English. **Voir l'exemple** (see the example):

Exemple: Oh no! I forgot my library book in our classroom. I need it for this weekend. Stay here. **Je vais à l'école!** I am going to the school!

1. We've got our suntan lotion, snorkels, towels, and snacks—we're ready.

   Nous **allons** **à la plage.** We are going to the beach.

2. How many of you have subway tickets? How about a map of downtown?

   Are you at least planning to visit some cool museums? No? That's too bad!

   Vous **allez** **à la ville!** It doesn't happen that often!
   You are going to the city!

3. **Fred** **va** **à la maison**—he's had enough of work!
   Fred is going home!

4. What's with all of your camping gear? Oh! I see. **Tu vas** *or* **Vous allez**

   à la montagne. You are going to the mountain.

5. **Aujourd'hui Alexandre** **va** **à l'école.** It's his first time, so he's very nervous! Today Alexandre is going to school.

6. **Il** **va** **à la foire avec son âne sur sa tête?**

   Il est fou (crazy)! He is going to the fair with his donkey on his head? He's crazy!

TEACHER'S NOTE

The translations have been supplied in the answer key in case students want to check their understanding of the sentences.

Dictée!

Listen to the audio file [02_06/Tr. 13] of the **dictée** for this **chapitre**. On the lines provided, write down the three sentences you hear. You do not need to write translations for them, though it's good practice to think through what the English translation would be. You may stop and repeat the audio file several times as you're writing down the sentences.

1. **Le loup va aux champs.**

   Translation: The wolf is going to the fields.

2. **Nous allons à la foire dans notre village.**

   Translation: We are going to the fair in our village.

3. **Le berger porte un chapeau bizarre.**

   Translation: The shepherd is wearing a bizarre hat.

Say It Aloud!

There are three things that you need to do to each of the following sentences:

1. Make the sentence *negative*. (Of course, the rule you just learned for **pas de** will not apply everywhere; it is used only when there is **un**, **une**, or **des** right after the verb.)
2. Translate the *negative* sentence into English.
3. Go back and pronounce the *negative* French sentence you created in step one, comparing your pronunciation to the audio file (03_05/Tr. 18). An example is provided below.

***Exemple:* Nous commençons un jeu.**
We are starting a game.

Negative: Nous ne commençons pas de jeu.

Translation: We are not starting a game.

RAPPEL

In this example, the word **un** was changed to **de** because the sentence is *negative*.

1. **Nous portons des vêtements intéressants.** We are wearing interesting clothes.

   Negative: Nous ne portons pas de vêtements intéressants.

   Translation: We are not wearing interesting clothes.

2. **Notre chat mange notre pain!** Our cat is eating our bread!

   Negative: Notre chat ne mange pas notre pain!

   Translation: Our cat is not eating our bread!

3. **Je porte mon fromage dans un sac.** I carry my cheese in a bag.

   Negative: Je ne porte pas mon fromage dans un sac.

   Translation: I do not carry my cheese in a bag.

4. **Tu chantes comme un oiseau.** You sing like a bird.

   Negative: Tu ne chantes pas comme un oiseau.

   Translation: You do not sing like a bird.

5. **Elle nage comme un poisson.** She swims like a fish.

   Negative: **Elle ne nage pas comme un poisson.**

   Translation: **She does not swim like a fish.**

6. **Ils ont l'air gentil.** They seem nice.

   Negative: **Ils n'ont pas l'air gentil.**

   Translation: **They do not seem nice.**

7. **Vous travaillez beaucoup.** You work a lot.

   Negative: **Vous ne travaillez pas beaucoup.**

   Translation: **You do not work a lot.**

Negative Mess

Put the words in the following sentences back in the correct order before you translate them into English.

1. **loup Le ville ne va à la pas.**

   Correct Order: **Le loup ne va pas à la ville.**

   Translation: **The wolf is not going to the city.**

2. **pantalon Le n' pas a de loup.**

   Correct Order: **Le loup n'a pas de pantalon.**

   Translation: **The wolf doesn't have pants.**

3. **l'air Le n' gentil pas loup a très.**

   Correct Order: **Le loup n'a pas l'air très gentil.**

   Translation: **The wolf doesn't seem very nice.**

4. **champs Aurélie pas ne va aux.**

   Correct Order: **Aurélie ne va pas aux champs.**

   Translation: **Aurélie is not going to the fields.**

5. **pas Jean n'ont Aurélie peur et du loup.**

   Correct Order: **Aurélie et Jean n'ont pas peur du loup.**

   Translation: **Aurélie and Jean are not afraid of the wolf.**

6. **"sommes Nous bêtes ne pas!"** say Jean and Aurélie in unison.

   Correct Order: **"Nous ne sommes pas bêtes!"**

   Translation: **"We are not dumb!"**

7. **"Vous berger ne que je suis pensez pas?"** asks the wolf.

   Correct Order: **"Vous pensez que je ne suis pas berger?"** *or* **"Vous ne pensez pas que je suis berger?"**

   Translation: **"You think that I'm not a shepherd?"** *or* **"You do not think that I am a shepherd?"**

Grammaire

Circle the correct answer.

1. To say, "You seem bizarre" in French, you'd say:

   a. **"Tu as air bizarre."**

   b. **"Tu as un air bizarre."**

   (c.) **"Tu as l'air bizarre."**

   d. **"Tu es l'air bizarre."**

2. If a French person asked you to join him for an appetizer of **escargots** (**un escargot** = a snail; pronounced *ES-KAR-GO*), you would probably say:

   a. **"Je ne pas manger des escargots."**

   b. **"Je ne mange des escargots."**

   c. **"Je mange ne des escargots."**

   (d.) **"Je ne mange pas d'escargots."**

   (Then again, you might say yes if you were adventurous . . . they're great with butter!)

3. If your neighbors insisted they had found your dog, but your family only owned cats, you could protest:

   (a.) "**Nous n'avons pas de chien!**"

   b. "**Nous ne avons pas de chien!**"

   c. "**Nous navons pas de chien!**"

   d. "**Notre chien ne voyage pas!**"

4. The wolf in our tale is not wearing a real coat, like a shepherd would, of course; he is wearing something more like a big old bag. How could we say, "He's not wearing a coat"?

   a. "**Il ne porte pas un manteau.**"

   (b.) "**Il ne porte pas de manteau.**"

   c. "**Il ne porte pas manteau.**"

   d. "**Il ne porte pas les manteaux.**"

Nouveau Vocabulaire

Fill in the blank with the correct translation(s) for each word.

Français	Anglais
1. avoir l'air (de), j'ai l'air (de)	to seem (like), I seem (like)
2. commencer, je commence	to begin/to start, I begin/I start
3. des vêtements	clothes
4. un sac	a bag
5. une patte	a paw/hoof/foot
6. une queue	a tail
7. une manière	a way, a manner
8. le pain	bread
9. ce	this, that
10. comme	like

Ancien Vocabulaire

Fill in the blank with the correct translation(s) for each word.

Français	Anglais
1. qui?	who?
2. un chapeau	a hat
3. quoi?	what?
4. où?	where?
5. un endroit	a place
6. réussir, je réussis	to succeed, I succeed
7. le genou	the knee

Français	Anglais
8. **pourquoi?**	why?
9. **porter, je porte***	to carry, I carry *or* to wear, I wear
10. **comment?**	how? *or* excuse me?

*Be sure to include both meanings of this word!

Negatives, Part I

Circle the best *negative* response to the following questions. Then, translate that response.

Exemple: **Tu as envie d'aller à la plage?** Do you feel like going to the beach?

a. **Non, je ne pas ai envie d'aller à la plage.**

b. **Non, j'ai ne pas envie d'aller à la plage.**

(c.) **Non, je n'ai pas envie d'aller à la plage.**

Translation: No, I don't feel like going to the beach.

1. **Le fromage est dans le sac?** The cheese is in the bag?/Is the cheese in the bag?

   a. **Non, le fromage nest pas dans le sac.**

   b. **Non, le fromage est pas dans le sac.**

   (c.) **Non, le fromage n'est pas dans le sac.**

   Translation: No, the cheese is not in the bag.

2. **Ta sœur commence à l'école aujourd'hui?** Your sister begins at school today?/ Does your sister begin at school today?

   (a.) **Non, ma sœur ne commence pas à l'école aujourd'hui.**

   b. **Non, ma sœur commence pas à l'école aujourd'hui.**

   c. **Non, ma sœur ne commence à l'école aujourd'hui.**

   Translation: No, my sister does not begin at school today.

3. **Votre chien a sept pattes!?** Your dog has seven paws!?/Does your dog have seven paws!?

   a. **Non, notre chien n'a sept pattes!**

   b. **Non, notre chien n'ont pas sept pattes!**

   (c.) **Non, notre chien n'a pas sept pattes!**

   Translation: No, our dog does not have seven paws!

4. **Le pain a l'air délicieux?** The bread seems delicious?/Does the bread seem delicious?

   a. **Non, le pain ne pas a l'air délicieux.**

   b. **Non, le pain a ne pas l'air délicieux.**

   ⓒ **Non, le pain n'a pas l'air délicieux.**

   Translation: No, the bread does not seem delicious.

Negatives, Part 2

In this last section, you no longer have the choice of three answers. You must create the answer yourself. That is, don't just rephrase the question—answer it negatively! After you write the *negative* response in French, translate it into English in the space provided.

1. **Tu aimes ma manière de chanter?** You like my way of singing?/ Do you like my way of singing?

   Negative Answer: Non, je n'aime pas ta manière de chanter.

   Translation: No, I don't like your way of singing.

2. **Vous portez des nouveaux vêtements?** You are wearing new clothes?/ Are you wearing new clothes?

   Negative Answer: Non, nous ne portons pas de nouveaux vêtements.

   Translation: No, we do not wear/we're not wearing new clothes.

3. **Je mange comme un cochon?** I eat like a pig?/Do I eat like a pig?

   Negative Answer: Non, tu ne manges pas comme un cochon.

   Translation: No, you don't eat/aren't eating like a pig.

Dictée!

Listen to the audio file [03_06/Tr. 19] of the **dictée** for this **chapitre**. On the lines provided, write down the three sentences you hear. You do not need to write translations for them, though it's good practice to think through what the English translation would be. You may stop and repeat the audio file several times as you're writing down the sentences.

1. Vous ne travaillez pas! Translation: You are not working!

2. Vous n'avez pas envie de travailler? Translation: You do not feel like working?

3. Les moutons ont l'air bêtes. Translation: The sheep seem dumb.

Question Words

Fill in the English equivalents of the French question words in the following chart.

Question Word	Anglais	Question Word	Anglais
comment?	how?	**pourquoi?**	why?
combien?	how many? *or* how much?	**où?**	where?
quoi?	what?	**quand?**	when?
qui?	who?		

Question Confusion

The following are several French questions that are all mixed up. Put them back in order and translate them.

1. **lac le est Où?**

   Correct Order: Où est le lac?

   Translation: Where is the lake?

2. **français tu Est-ce que es?**

   Correct Order: Est-ce que tu es français?

   Translation: Are you French?

3. **Est-ce qu' fatigués sont ils?**

   Correct Order: Est-ce qu'ils sont fatigués?

   Translation: Are they tired?

4. **vas Est-ce que tu au marché?**

   Correct Order: Est-ce que tu vas au marché?

   Translation: Are you going to the market?

5. **choses Combien achètes de tu est-ce que?**

   Correct Order: Combien de choses est-ce que tu achètes?

   Translation: How many things are you buying?

6. **marché le termine est-ce que Quand?**

   Correct Order: **Quand est-ce que le marché termine?**

   Translation: **When does the market finish?**

7. **est-ce que Pourquoi allez vous au marché?**

   Correct Order: **Pourquoi est-ce que vous allez au marché?**

   Translation: **Why are you going to the market?**

Ask It Aloud! The Gatekeeper's Checklist

The following is a list of questions that the **le gardien** (the gatekeeper/guard) of the village normally asks people trying to enter. Translate the questions into French. For this exercise, always use the **vous** form for "you," especially since **le gardien** doesn't normally know the people who are coming into the town. Then, go back and practice asking each French question aloud. Check your pronunciation with the audio file (04_05/Tr. 24).

1. Why are you here?

   Translation: **Pourquoi est-ce que vous êtes ici?**

2. Where are you going in the village?

   Translation: **Où est-ce que vous allez dans le village?**

3. Are you staying here?

   Translation: **Est-ce que vous restez ici?**

4. How many animals do you have?

   Translation: **Combien d'animaux est-ce que vous avez?**

5. How are you traveling?

   Translation: **Comment est-ce que vous voyagez?**

6. Do you have friends here?

   Translation: **Est-ce que vous avez des amis ici?**

Rappel

Listen closely to the pronunciation of **est-ce que** on the audio file for this **chapitre**'s opening dialogue (04_01/Tr. 20), either by itself, or combined with a question word. The letter **t** is silent! In fact, the two words **est-ce** often end up blending together into one long sound—like saying the letter *s*.

Grammaire

1. If you hear a French speaker ask you a question beginning with "**Est-ce que . . .** " you know that she is:
   (a.) looking for a yes or no answer.
   b. looking for you to tell her the *reason* for something.
   c. looking for you to respond with **parce que**.
   d. looking for trouble.
2. To ask, "Why are the cats eating flowers?" you would say:
   a. "**Pourquoi les chats est-ce que mangent des fleurs?**"
   b. "**Pourquoi mangent les chats est-ce que des fleurs?**"
   (c.) "**Pourquoi est-ce que les chats mangent des fleurs?**"
   d. "**Est-ce que les chats mangent des fleurs?**"
3. To ask, "Why do the cats eat flowers?" you would say:
   a. "**Pourquoi les chats est-ce que mangent des fleurs?**"
   b. "**Pourquoi mangent les chats est-ce que des fleurs?**"
   (c.) "**Pourquoi est-ce que les chats mangent des fleurs?**"
   d. "**Est-ce que les chats mangent des fleurs?**"

4. To ask "Why is the cat eating flowers?" you would say:
   a. "**Pourquoi le chat est-ce que mange des fleurs?**"
   b. "**Pourquoi mange le chat est-ce que des fleurs?**"
   (c.) "**Pourquoi est-ce que le chat mange des fleurs?**"
   d. "**Est-ce que le chat mange des fleurs?**"
5. Considering your answers to questions 2, 3, and 4, it is clear that **Pourquoi est-ce que . . .** can mean:
   a. Why do . . .
   b. Why are . . .
   (c.) Why do . . . ? *and* Why are . . . ? *and* Why is . . . ?
   d. Why is . . .

Nouveau Vocabulaire

Fill in the blank with the correct translation for each word.

Français	Anglais
1. acheter, j'achète	to buy, I buy
2. entrer, j'entre	to enter, I enter
3. être d'accord, je suis d'accord	to agree, I agree
4. terminer, je termine	to terminate/finish, I terminate/finish
5. le marché	the market
6. un fruit	a fruit
7. un légume	a vegetable
8. une chose	a thing
9. fatigué	tired
10. encore	again

Ancien Vocabulaire

Fill in the blank with the correct translation for each word.

Français	Anglais
1. le dos	the back
2. avoir l'air (de), j'ai l'air (de)	to seem (like), I seem (like)
3. une chaussette	a sock
4. une chaussure	a shoe
5. jaune	yellow
6. vert	green

Français	Anglais
7. **laisser, je laisse**[4]	to leave (something or someone), I leave (something or someone)
8. **le fleuve**	the river
9. **le lac**	the lake
10. **la plage**	the beach

Question Pileup

Behold, a tragic situation: The sentences are all crunched together after a gigantic question pileup. See if you can separate each line into distinct words again to form a clear question. Then, translate that question into English. We've provided you with an example:

Exemple: **Pourquoiest-cequ'ilportesonânesurlatête?**

Question: **Pourquoi est-ce qu'il porte son âne sur la tête?**

Translation: **Why is he carrying his donkey on his head?**

1. **Oùestlemarché?**

   Question: **Où est le marché?**

   Translation: **Where is the market?**

2. **Combiend'animauxavez-vous?**

   Question: **Combien d'animaux avez-vous?**

   Translation: **How many animals do you have?**

3. **Quandest-cequ'ellevaàlamaison?**

   Question: **Quand est-ce qu'elle va à la maison?**

   Translation: **When is she going to the house?**

4. You learned in *FFCA* **chapitre** 13 that **laisser** does not mean to simply leave a location—it means to leave behind an object, person, etc. In **chapitre** 9 of this book you'll learn a verb that does mean simply "to leave a location": **partir**.

4. **Pourquoiest-cequ'ilslaissentleurfromageici?**

   Question: Pourquoi est-ce qu'ils laissent leur fromage ici?

   Translation: Why do they leave their cheese here?

5. **Est-cequ'elleaimesonécole?**

   Question: Est-ce qu'elle aime son école?

   Translation: Does she like her school?

6. **Pourquoicherchez-vouslaville?**

   Question: Pourquoi cherchez-vous la ville?

   Translation: Why are you looking for the city?

7. **Commentest-cequevousallezauvillage?**

   Question: Comment est-ce que vous allez au village?

   Translation: How are you going to the village?

Questions about Jean et Aurélie

Use your knowledge of French questions to choose the best response to each of the following questions. Many of the choices (a, b, c, d) are *true* statements about the story of Jean and Aurélie, but only one of those choices will clearly respond to the question, so be sure to circle the correct response.

1. **Comment est-ce que Jean, Aurélie, le meunier, et Thibault vont au village?**
   How are Jean, Aurélie, the miller, and Thibault going to the village?
   a. **Ils ont une voiture.** They have a car.

   b. **Ils vont aujourd'hui.** They go/are going today.

   (c.) **Ils marchent.** They walk/are walking.

   d. **L'âne du meunier porte Jean, Aurélie, et Thibault sur son dos.**
   The miller's donkey carries/is carrying Jean, Aurélie, and Thibault on its back.

2. **Pourquoi est-ce que Thibault va avec Jean et Aurélie?**
   Why is Thibault going with Jean and Aurélie?
   a. **Il marche.** He walks/is walking.

   (b.) **Il a envie de voir la ville.** He wants to see the city.

   c. **Il a deux amis.** He has two friends.

   d. **Il va avec une souris et une vache.** He goes/is going with a mouse and a cow.

3. **Est-ce que le gardien [gatekeeper/guard] du village a un chien?**
Does the gatekeeper of the village have a dog?
   (a.) **Oui, et il s'appelle** (his name is) **Bruno.** Yes, and his name is Bruno.

   b. **Non. Bruno n'a pas de chien.** No, Bruno doesn't have a dog.

   c. **Non. Le gardien [gatekeeper/guard] n'a pas de chien.** No, the gatekeeper doesn't have a dog.

   d. **Non. Bruno n'est pas le gardien.** No, Bruno is not the gatekeeper.

4. **Où vont Jean et Aurélie?**
Where are Jean and Aurélie going?
   (a.) **Au zoo.** To the zoo.

   b. **Le fromage.** The cheese.

   c. **Une souris et une vache.** A mouse and a cow.

   d. **À la montagne.** To the mountain.

5. **Le meunier a beaucoup d'enfants. Combien d'enfants est-ce qu'il a?**
The miller has many children. How many children does he have?
   (a.) **Quatre.** Four.

   b. **Il aime beaucoup ses enfants.** He likes his children very much.

   c. **Dans le village.** In the village.

   d. **Ils ont des yeux verts.** They have green eyes.

Dictée!

Listen to the audio file [04_06/Tr. 25] of the **dictée** for this **chapitre**. On the lines provided, write down the three sentences you hear. You do not need to write translations for them, though it's good practice to think through what the English translation would be. You may stop and repeat the audio file several times as you're writing down the sentences.

1. **Est-ce que tu es fatigué?**

   Translation: Are you tired?

2. **Pourquoi est-ce que tu ne manges pas tes légumes?**

   Translation: Why aren't you eating your vegetables?

3. **Il n'est pas d'accord avec moi.**

   Translation: He does not agree with me.

CHAPITRE 5 CINQ

Here we are at the end of an exciting unit! You've learned how to say, "I am" (**je suis**) and "I go" (**je vais**) using two extremely common verbs. To boot, you figured out how to say, "I am not!" and "I'm not going!" thanks to our **chapitre** on negatives using **ne** and **pas**. You also started to see how to ask questions in French with the famous expression **est-ce que**, accompanied by our seven question words, and also by using inversion. Before reviewing these concepts in more detail, it's time to take a deep breath and . . . keep breathing in . . . a little bit more . . . now *quick*! Recite all of your vocabulary words as you exhale! (Don't forget to breathe when you need to, though—we wouldn't want you passing out.)

French	English
☐ **être, je suis**	to be, I am
☐ **voyager, je voyage**	to travel, I travel
☐ **visiter, je visite**	to visit, I visit
☐ **avoir envie de, j'ai envie de**	to feel like/to want, I feel like/I want
☐ **un endroit**	a place
☐ **une idée**	an idea
☐ **ensemble**	together
☐ **intelligent/bête**	smart/dumb
☐ **content/triste**	happy/sad
☐ **difficile/simple**	difficult/simple
☐ **aller, je vais**	to go, I go
☐ **un manteau**	a coat

French	English
☐ **un chapeau**	a hat
☐ **une chemise**	a shirt
☐ **un pantalon**	pants
☐ **une chaussure/chaussette**	a shoe, a sock
☐ **un mouton**	a sheep
☐ **un berger**	a shepherd
☐ **une foire**	a fair
☐ **un loup**	a wolf
☐ **avoir l'air (de), j'ai l'air (de)**	to seem (like), I seem (like)
☐ **commencer, je commence**	to begin/to start, I begin/I start
☐ **des vêtements**	clothes
☐ **un sac**	a bag
☐ **une patte**	a paw

French	English
☐ une queue	a tail
☐ une manière	a way, a manner
☐ le pain	bread
☐ ce	this, that
☐ comme	like
☐ acheter, j'achète	to buy, I buy
☐ entrer, j'entre	to enter, I enter
☐ être d'accord, je suis d'accord	to agree, I agree

French	English
☐ terminer, je termine	to terminate/finish, I terminate/finish
☐ le marché	the market
☐ un fruit	a fruit
☐ un légume	a vegetable
☐ une chose	a thing
☐ fatigué	tired
☐ encore	again

My List of Words to Master

So that you can easily review the words you are having difficulty remembering, write them down on the lines provided below.

Grammaire

The Verb *Être* ("to be," Chapitre 1)

Conjugation

Fill in the chart below with the conjugated forms of the verb **être** (to be).

Person	Singular	Plural
1st Person	je suis (I am)	nous sommes (we are)
2nd Person	tu es (you are)	vous êtes (you are)
3rd Person	il/elle est (he/she/it is)	ils/elles sont (they are)

Eavesdropping

Let's pretend we're listening in on a couple of conversations between French speakers. Translate their conversations in the space provided on the right. Then, listen to the conversations on the audio file (05_01/Tr. 26).

1. *The Unhappy Pair*

"Je suis content."
Translation: "I am happy."

"Pourquoi est-ce que tu es content?"
Translation: "Why are you happy?"

"Parce que nous sommes ensemble!"
Translation: "Because we are together!"

"Vraiment? Je suis triste."
Translation: "Really? I am sad."

"Pourquoi est-ce que tu es triste?"
Translation: "Why are you sad?"

"Parce que tu es méchant!"
Translation: "Because you are mean!"

2. *Look on the Bright Side*

"Voilà! Nous sommes à la mer!"
Translation: "There we go! We are at the sea!"

"Non, non, Monsieur! Vous êtes au lac. Le lac est petit, il n'est pas grand!"
Translation: "No, no, sir! You are at the lake. The lake is small; it is not large!"

"Mais la mer est bleue!"
Translation: "But the sea is blue!"

"Oui, monsieur, mais le lac est aussi bleu. Donc [therefore *or* so], **c'est un lac."**
Translation: "Yes, sir, but the lake is also blue. So, it's a lake."

"D'accord, d'accord, [OK, OK] **mais la mer a une plage!"**
Translation: "OK, OK, but the sea has a beach!"

"Oui, mais le lac a aussi une plage!"
Translation: "Yes, but the lake also has a beach!"

"Mais . . . alors, où est le lac?"
Translation: "But . . . so then, where is the lake?"

"Le lac est dans la forêt."
Translation: "The lake is in the forest."

"Et où est la forêt?"
Translation: "And where is the forest?"

"La forêt est à côté des champs."
Translation: "The forest is next to the fields."

"Et où sont les champs?"
Translation: "And where are the fields?"

"Les champs sont près des montagnes."
Translation: "The fields are near the mountains."

"Et où sont les montagnes?"
Translation: "And where are the mountains?"

"Ben, les montagnes sont à côté de la mer."
Translation: "Well, the mountains are next to the sea."

"Donc, nous sommes près de la mer!"
Translation: "So, we're near the sea!"

The Verb *Aller* ("to go," Chapitre 2)

Conjugation

Fill in the chart below with the conjugated forms of the verb **aller**, "to go." Be sure to translate the phrase from the **chapitre** 2 Conversation Journal as well.

Person	Singular	Plural
1st Person	je vais (I go)	nous allons (we go)
2nd Person	tu vas (you go)	vous allez (you go)
3rd Person	il/elle va (he/she goes)	ils/elles vont (they go)
—	Vas-y! Allez-y! Go ahead!/Go on!/Keep going!	

Three Strikes and They're Out!

Out of the following five sentences, three contain mistakes. Your job is to cross out each of the mistakes and then write the corrected sentence in the space provided. But be careful! The three sentences with mistakes might have more than one mistake in each sentence! Once you've fixed all of the mistakes, translate *all* of the sentences.

1. **Aujourd'hui, nous allons à la plage.**

   Corrected Sentence: No mistakes.

   Translation: Today, we are going to the beach.

2. **Vous ~~aller à le~~ zoo?**

   Corrected Sentence: Vous allez au zoo?

   Translation: You are going to the zoo?

3. **Je ~~vas~~ à la maison.**

   Corrected Sentence: Je vais à la maison.

   Translation: I am going to the house.

4. **Elle va au marché.**

   Corrected Sentence: No mistakes.

   Translation: She is going to the market.

5. **Tu ~~vais à les champs avec les moutons~~?**

   Corrected Sentence: Tu vas aux champs avec les moutons?

   Translation: You are going to the fields with the sheep?

Negation with *Ne* and *Pas* (Chapitre 3)

Go Fish . . . for Negatives!

The following four sentences are missing some negative words (**ne**, **n'**, **pas**, or **de**). Fish around in the pond below and stick the right words in the blanks in order to complete the sentences by making them negative. Then translate the sentences into English in the space provided below. (Hint: You can cross off a negative word every time you use it.)

1. **Aurelie et Jean** __ne__ **sont** __pas__ **au zoo.**

   Translation: Aurélie and Jean are not going to the zoo.

2. **Le loup** __ne__ **porte** __pas__ __de__ **chaussures.**

   Translation: The wolf is not wearing shoes.

3. **La mère de Thibault** __n'__ **a** __pas__ __de__ **fromage.**

   Translation: Thibault's mother does not have cheese.

4. **Vous** __n'__ **allez** __pas__ **à la montagne?**

   Translation: You are not going to the mountain?

5. **Je** __ne__ **vais** __pas__ **à la maison.**

   Translation: I am not going to the house.

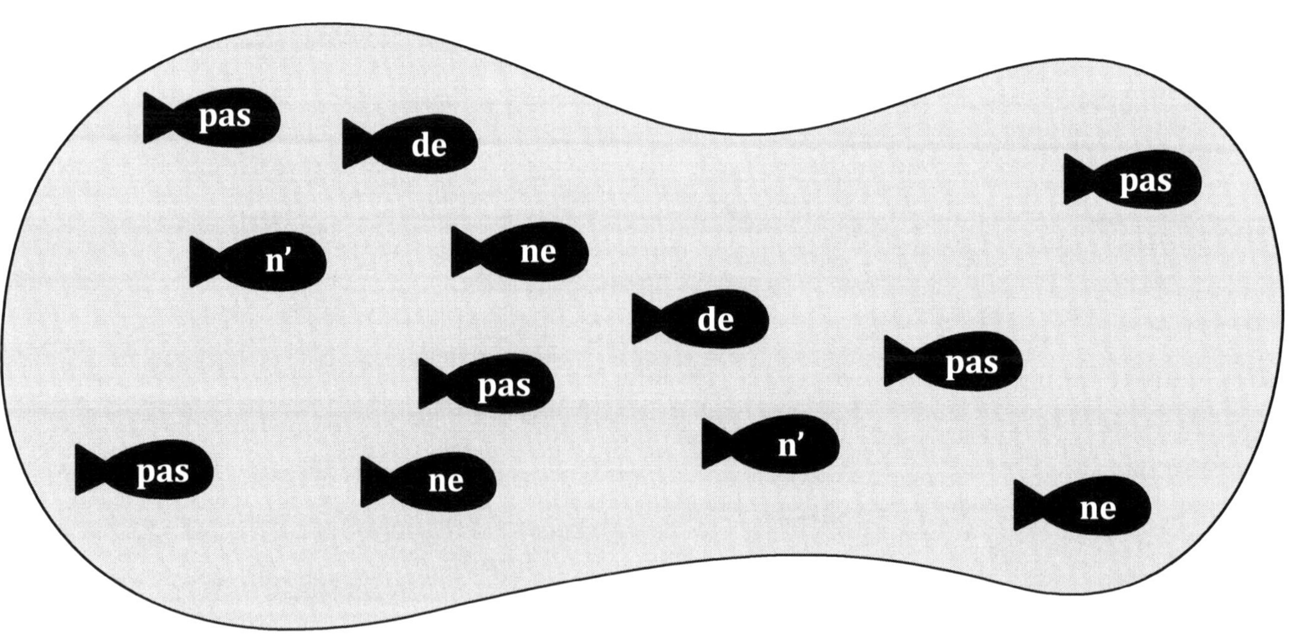

Questions: *Est-ce Que* (Chapitre 4)

You Ask the Questions!

In this last review exercise, it's your turn to ask questions for once. We provide you with an answer, and you must create a question that would produce that answer. The kind of question word you should use is to the right of the answer, in parentheses. As you see in the following example, we give you the answer as a statement: "We have three brothers." Using the kind of question listed in parentheses, you must come up with the question that produces the statement.

Exemple:

Nous avons trois frères. (How many?) **We have three brothers.**
Question: **Combien de frères est-ce que vous avez?**
How many brothers do you have?

1. **Je vais à la ville à trois heures** [three o'clock]. (When?)
   I go/I'm going to the city at three o'clock.
   Question: **Quand est-ce que tu vas à la ville?**
   When do you go/are you doing to the city?
2. **Ils travaillent au marché.** (Where?)
   They work/are working at the market.
   Question: **Où est-ce qu'ils travaillent?**
   Where do they work/are they working?
3. **Elle achète une chemise pour l'anniversaire [birthday] de sa mère.** (Why?)
   She is buying a shirt for her mother's birthday.
   Question: **Pourquoi est-ce qu'elle achète une chemise?**
   Why is she buying a shirt?
4. **Nous allons au village avec la voiture.** (How?)
   We go/are going to the village with the car.
   Question: **Comment est-ce que vous allez au village?**
   How do you go/are you going to the village?

Chant-Confused Conjugation

Go back to the beginning of this chapter and study the chant of the verb **faire** for a few minutes before you try to do this exercise. Then, do your best to put this chart of conjugations of the verb **faire** back in the correct order by crossing out the incorrect forms and replacing them with the correct ones. If any of the forms are correct, you can leave them that way.

Person	Singular	Plural
1st Person	**je ~~faisons~~** fais (I do/I make)	**nous ~~fais~~** faisons (we do/we make)
2nd Person	**tu ~~fait~~** fais (you do/you make)	**vous ~~font~~** faites (you do/you make
3rd Person	**il/elle ~~fais~~** fait (he/she/it does; he/she/it makes)	**ils/elles ~~faites~~** font (they do/they make)

A Conversation with the Fox

After slipping away from the gourmet rats, Jean, Aurélie, and Thibault cross paths with the fox, who is on the hunt for something. Imagine that the questions to the left are what the fox asks the three travelers. Match the appropriate response on the right to each question on the left by drawing a line between them:

C 1. **"Qui êtes-vous?"** Who are you?

A 2. **"Qu'est-ce que vous faites ici?"** What are you doing here?

E 3. **"Qu'est-ce que vous achetez au marché?"** What are you buying at the market?

D 4. **"Qui cache mon œuf?!"** Who is hiding my egg?

B 5. **"Où sont les rats!?"** Where are the rats!?

A. "We're just here to do some shopping."

B. "Not sure. Probably somewhere around here. . . . Excuse us . . . gotta go!"

C. "I'm Jean, and this is Aurélie and Thibault."

D. "I haven't seen any *people* around here with it . . . "

E. "Oh, uh, nothing—fruits, vegetables . . . no eggs, though!"

Ask It Aloud!

Translate the following questions into French, and then try asking them out loud. Compare your pronunciation to the audio file (06_05/Tr. 31).

1. When is the fox arriving?

   Quand est-ce que le renard arrive?

2. What are they doing with the egg?

   Qu'est-ce qu'ils font avec l'œuf?

3. Why are you (**vous**) hiding an egg?

   Pourquoi est-ce que vous cachez l'oeuf?

4. What is he doing with his tail?

   Qu'est-ce qu'il fait avec sa queue?

5. Who eats a cake with fish heads?

   Qui mange un gâteau avec des têtes de poissons?! *or* **Qui est-ce qui mange un gâteau avec des têtes de poissons?**

Grammaire

Circle the correct answer.

1. In French, the verb **faire** can mean:

   a. to do and to finish.
   b. to make and to finish.
   (c.) to do and to make.
   d. to have and to hold.

2. Identify one question below that would *never* happen using the question word "what" in French:

   (a.) **Quoi est-ce que tu fais?**
   b. **Qu'est-ce qu'il mange?**
   c. **Vous parlez de quoi?**
   d. **Qu'est-ce que tu cherches?**

3. What is the difference between the question **"Qui nage dans le lac?"** and the question **"Qui est-ce qui nage dans le lac?"**

   a. The first question asks, "Who is swimming in the lake?" and the second asks, "Who does swim in the lake?"
   b. The first question asks, "What is swimming in the lake?" and the second asks, "Who is swimming in the lake?"
   (c.) There is no difference in meaning.
   d. The first question asks, "Who is swimming in the lake?" and the second asks, "What is swimming in the lake?"

Nouveau Vocabulaire

Fill in the blank with the correct translation for each word.

Français	Anglais
1. **faire, je fais**	to do/make, I do/make
2. **arriver, j'arrive**	to arrive, I arrive
3. **cacher, je cache**	to hide (something), I hide (something)
4. **casser, je casse**	to break, I break
5. **tirer, je tire**	to pull, I pull
6. **dégoûtant**	disgusting
7. **l'œuf**	the egg
8. **l'omelette**	the omelet
9. **le rat**	the rat
10. **la dame**	the lady

Ancien Vocabulaire

Fill in the blank with the correct translation for each word.

Français	Anglais
1. **l'arbre**	the tree
2. **une sœur**	a sister
3. **une fille**	a girl, a daughter
4. **espérer [que], j'espère [que]**	to hope [that], I hope [that]
5. **rester, je reste**	to stay, I stay
6. **avoir peur de, j'ai peur de**	to be afraid of, I am afraid of
7. **une femme**	a woman, a wife
8. **une mère**	a mother
9. **entrer, j'entre**	to enter, I enter
10. **être d'accord, je suis d'accord**	to agree, I agree

Lost Questions

In the left-hand column, you will see questions—or at least, the beginnings of questions—whose ends have been smudged and faded so that we will never know exactly what they're asking. In the right-hand column, though, you will see possible answers to all of the different questions. Using just your knowledge of question words, draw a line to the answer on the right that *could* be connected to the question on the left.

Answer	Question	Possible answer
D	1. **Quand est-ce que je . . .** When do I . . .	A. **Dans la grange.** In the barn.
F	2. **Qui est-ce qui va . . .** Who is going . . .	B. **Parce que nous allons à la ville.** Because we are going to the city.
A	3. **Où est la . . .** Where is the . . .	C. **Deux.** Two.
B	4. **Pourquoi est-ce que vous . . .** Why are you . . .	D. **Tu travailles aujourd'hui.** You are working today.
E	5. **Qu'est-ce qu'il . . .** What is he . . .	E. **Il fait une omelette.** He is making an omelette.
G	6. **Comment est-ce que tu . . .** How do you . . .	F. **Jean.**
C	7. **Combien de rats . . .** How many rats . . .	G. **Je réussis parce que j'étudie!** I succeed because I study!

Traduction

In this **chapitre**'s dialogue with Jean, Aurélie, and Thibault, there are six (and only six) questions containing our famous question expression **est-ce que**. Take a glance back at the dialogue and do the following:

1. Rewrite the questions, in French, on the lines provided.
2. Then, translate each sentence.

1. Question: Est-ce que vous regardez les deux rats là-bas?

   ____

   Translation: Are you looking at the two rats over there?

   ____

Rappel

As you write the French versions down, think about all you've learned about questions. What is **est-ce que**? How is it used? What is the correct order of the words in a question?

2. Question: **Qu'est-ce qu'ils font?**

   Translation: **What are they doing?**

3. Question: **Qu'est-ce que vous faites là?**

   Translation: **What are you doing there?**

4. Question: **Qu'est-ce que vous avez?**

   Translation: **What do you have?**

5. Question: **OK, mais pourquoi est-ce que tu es sur ton dos avec l'œuf dans les pattes?**

   Translation: **OK, but why are you on your back with the egg in your paws?**

6. Question: **Et pourquoi est-ce que tu tires ton ami par la queue?**

   Translation: **And why are you pulling your friend by the tail?**

Dictée!

Listen to the audio file [06_06/Tr. 32] of the **dictée** for this **chapitre**. On the lines provided, write down the three sentences you hear. You do not need to write translations for them, though it's good practice to think through what the English translation would be. You may stop and repeat the audio file several times as you're writing down the sentences.

1. **Qu'est-ce que vous faites?**

   Translation: What are you doing?

2. **Nous faisons nos devoirs.**

   Translation: We are doing our homework.

3. **Qui fait une omelette?**

   Translation: Who is making an omelet?

Signs

Below are messages on five different signs. Your job is to draw a line linking the sign with the appropriate place in the right-hand column where you would expect to find it. Then, translate the sign in the space provided.

1. **Vous ne devez pas jouer avec les serpents.**

   Translation: You should not/must not play with snakes.

2. **Vous pouvez acheter des légumes ici.**

   Translation: You can buy vegetables here.

3. **Vous ne devez pas parler.**

   Translation: You should not/must not speak/talk.

4. **Attention! Vous pouvez tomber!**

   Translation: Careful! You can fall!

5. **Vous ne devez pas marcher ici.**

   Translation: You should not/must not walk here.

A. the library

B. a major highway

C. a mountain trail

D. the zoo

E. the market

Interpreting at the Market

Below are bits of conversations that you might have heard at the market when Jean, Aurélie, Thibault, and his dad were there. If the sentence is in French, first read it out loud, and compare your pronunciation to the audio file (07_05/Tr. 37). If the sentence is in English, don't bother reading it aloud; just translate it right into French![2]

1. **Qu'est-ce que vous voulez, Monsieur!?**

   Translation: What do you want, sir!?

2. **Est-ce que je peux regarder vos fromages?**

   Translation: Can I look at your cheeses?

3. Can I have a peach?

   Translation: Est-ce que je peux avoir une pêche?

4. **Je dois acheter trois sacs de pommes de terre; je n'ai pas assez de pommes de terre à la maison.**

   Translation: I have to buy three bags of potatoes; I don't have enough potatoes at the house.

5. Does he want two tomatoes or three?

   Translation: Est-ce qu'il veut deux tomates ou trois?

6. **Est-que vous pouvez laisser un sac de fraises pour moi?**

   Translation: Can you leave a bag of strawberries for me?

7. We want two pigs, please!

   Translation: Nous voulons deux cochons, s'il vous plait!

Teacher's Note

Traditional English grammar rules dictate that the proper wording of this question would be "May I look at your cheeses?" However, since the second half of the nineteenth century, "can" has been used in informal contexts to denote permission, so in this context the use of "can" is appropriate.

2. Of course, we won't stop you if you really want to read them out loud, but you won't find any English answers on the audio file!

Grammaire

Circle the correct answer.

1. The verbs **devoir**, **pouvoir**, and **vouloir** are called "boot verbs" because:

   a. their meanings are all similar.
   b. they are all used in the same situations.
   c. if you write out their conjugations, they follow the same boot-shaped pattern.
   d. all boot verbs end in **-oir**, just as *all* non-boot verbs end in **-er**.
   e. they all come from Italy.

2. **Il peut . . .** is always translated as "He is able to . . ."

   a. true
   b. false, it can also be translated "he must"
   c. false, it can also be translated "he is willing to"
   d. false, it can also be translated "he can"

3. **Devoir**, **pouvoir**, and **vouloir** are often used as helping verbs. What do we call the form of the *other* verb that is "helped" by them? For example, what is the form of the underlined verb being helped by **pouvoir** in this sentence: **Est-ce que tu peux <u>chanter</u>?**

   a. the present tense
   b. the infinitive
   c. the helped verb
   d. the boot verb

4. Which of the following sentences correctly uses a boot verb *negatively*?

   a. **Il ne pas peut nager.**
   b. **Il ne peut nager pas.**
   c. **Il peut ne nager pas.**
   d. **Il ne peut pas nager.**

Nouveau Vocabulaire

Fill in the blank with the correct translation(s) for each word.

Français	Anglais
1. **devoir, je dois**	to have to, should; I have to, I should
2. **pouvoir, je peux**	to be able to, I can
3. **vouloir, je veux**	to want, I want
4. **cher**	expensive
5. **si**	so
6. **une pomme**	an apple
7. **une fraise**	a strawberry
8. **une pêche**	a peach
9. **une pomme de terre**	a potato
10. **une tomate**	a tomato

Ancien Vocabulaire

Fill in the blank with the correct translation(s) for each word.

Français	Anglais
1. **un cochon**	a pig
2. **un renard**	a fox
3. **un serpent**	a snake
4. **un oiseau**	a bird
5. **un cheval**	a horse
6. **un mouton**	a sheep
7. **un loup**	a wolf
8. **un rat**	a rat

Français	Anglais
9. **cacher, je cache**	to hide (something), I hide (something)
10. **casser, je casse**	to break, I break

Fais Tes Devoirs (Do Your Homework)

Remember, in *FFCA* **chapitre 2** you learned that **les devoirs** means "homework." **Devoir**, you learned in this **chapitre**, simply means "to have to" or "must." So you see, **les devoirs** are just things you *must* do, like this verb chart! We've filled in the first box for you.

Person	Singular	Plural
1st Person	**je dois** (I must)	nous devons (we must)
2nd Person	tu dois (you must)	vous devez (you must)
3rd Person	il/elle doit (he/she/it must)	ils/elles doivent (they must)

Which Helper?

To complete the following sentences, circle the correct helping verb from the choices underneath each blank.

1. What!? You haven't done your assignment yet? **Le cours (un cours** = a class) **commence dans quinze (15) minutes—tu ________________ faire tes devoirs!**
   (dois / peux / veux) [dois circled]
   The class begins in fifteen minutes—you should/have to/must do your homework![C]
2. That was the best movie I've seen all summer! I can't wait for it to be out of the theaters—**je ________________ acheter le DVD.** I want to buy the DVD.
   (dois / peux / veux) [veux circled]
3. I think we're going to miss the bus, but don't worry—the shop isn't far.
   Nous ________________ marcher là-bas. We can walk there.
   (devons / pouvons / voulons) [pouvons circled]

Teacher's Note

[C]Make sure your students justify their choice of translation for the verb **devoir**. If they choose "must" or "have to," ask them what makes it such a serious situation that they would make that choice. Or, if they choose "should," ask them what lessens the seriousness from something that is "mandatory" to something that would simply be a "good idea."

4. Hey! We've got an emergency over here!
   Est-ce que vous _________________ chercher la police!?
   (devez / (pouvez) / voulez) Can you look for the police!?

5. I can't go out tonight because my little brother is home, and I'm babysitting.
   Je _________________ être à la maison! I must/have to be at the house!
   ((dois) / peux / veux)

6. Most of the girls want to go surfing, so they'd rather not stay in town.
   Elles _________________ aller à la plage. They want to go to the beach.
   (doivent / peuvent / (veulent))

7. Huh? We have a test *tomorrow*!? **Nous _________________ étudier!** We must study!
   ((devons) / pouvons / voulons)

8. Sorry, lady, if your kids want to see giraffes and tigers, they're not going to get any of that here at our farm. **Ils _________________ aller au zoo.** They can/must/have to/should go to the zoo.[D]
   ((doivent) / peuvent / veulent)

9. We seem to be lost. **Est-ce que je _________________ regarder la carte, s'il te plaît?**
   (dois / (peux) / veux) Can I see the map, please?

10. Is your **grand-père** (grandfather) hungry now? We can find a restaurant whenever he wants. I'm afraid of him when he hasn't had enough to eat.

    Quand est-ce qu'il _________________ manger? When does he want to eat?
    (doit / peut / (veut))

Dictée!

Listen to the audio file [07_06/Tr. 38] of the **dictée** for this **chapitre**. On the lines provided, write down the three sentences you hear. You do not need to write translations for them, though it's good practice to think through what the English translation would be. You may stop and repeat the audio file several times as you're writing down the sentences.

1. **Je peux manger quatre pommes!** **Translation: I can eat four apples.**

2. **Ils doivent marcher à l'école.** **Translation: They have to walk to school.**

3. **Tu ne peux pas parler français?** **Translation: You cannot speak French?**

Teacher's Note

[D]Again, make sure your students justify their choice of translation for the verb **devoir**. If they choose "must" or "have to," ask them what makes it such a serious situation that they would make that choice. Or, if they choose "should," ask them what lessens the seriousness from something that is "mandatory" to something that would simply be a "good idea."

Quelle Heure Est-Il?

Quelle heure est-il? Five o'clock? Six o'clock? **Quelle heure est-il?** Are we on time? Did we miss the show? **Quelle heure est-il?** Aren't they open yet? When will everyone get here? **Quelle heure est-il?** Hmmm . . . maybe you've cracked this question by now—thanks to the **chant**, plus the different (but related!) questions in this paragraph. Did you guess that it means "What time is it?"

The question **Quelle heure est-il?** does not actually contain the word "time," as in our English expression, "What *time* is it?" Instead, in French we use the word **heure**, or "hour" in English, to ask, literally, "Which hour is it?"[2] And so the logical response includes the word **heure** as well!

Il est une heure.	It is one o'clock.
Il est huit heures.	It is eight o'clock.
Il est onze heures.	It is eleven o'clock.

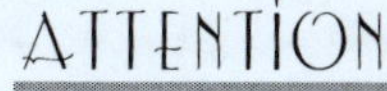

The word **heure** is usually plural (**heures**) since we're usually talking about a number larger than one. However, when it's one o'clock, we use the singular **heure** as you can see to the left. Either way, it all sounds the same, since the **s** in **heures** is not pronounced. So don't say too much!

If you want to say that you're doing something *at* five o'clock, or you're going somewhere *at* seven o'clock, all you need to do is throw in the little preposition **à** ("to" or "at") like this:

Je fais mes devoirs à cinq heures.
I do my homework at five o'clock.

Ta sœur arrive à deux heures.
Your sister is arriving at two o'clock.

Twelve O'Clock Rock

If you want to talk about something happening in the middle of the *day* (12:00 p.m.), you'd say **midi** in French: **Je mange à midi.**

On the other hand, if you're describing something in the middle of the *night* (12:00 a.m.), you'd say **minuit**: **Je ne mange pas à minuit! Je dors!**

2. Again, as with some other expressions we've learned—for example, the Curious Haves—the French way of speaking (saying "Which hour is it?" instead of "What time is it?") may seem bizarre to us who speak English; but, to a French speaker, asking "What time is it?" will seem bizarre, too!

"My friends are afraid of your snake. They think he's dangerous."

"Ils ont raison. Il est très dangereux! C'est un cobra."
"They are right. It's very dangerous. It's a cobra."

Finally, as a refresher, try your hand at filling in the **avoir** chart below. It is like a normal verb chart, but you have to factor in whether or not you should add **raison** or **tort** to the form of **avoir**. We've filled in one box for you, and the answers are upside down at the bottom of the page.

Avoir Raison ou Tort?

Person	Singular	Plural
1st Person	____j'ai raison____ (I am right)[A]	____nous avons tort____ (we are wrong)[B]
2nd Person	**tu as tort** (you are wrong)	____vous avez raison____ (you are right)[C]
3rd Person	____il a raison____ (he is right)[D] ____elle a tort____ (she is wrong)[E]	____ils ont raison____ (they are wrong)[F]

[A]j'ai raison [B]nous avons tort [C]vous avez raison [D]il a raison [E]elle a tort [F]ils ont raison

Quelle Heure Est-Il?

Look at the five clocks below. Say what time it is out loud in French and check your pronunciation against the audio file (08_05/Tr. 43). Then, write the sentences out in French in the space provided underneath the clocks.

1.	2.	3.	4.	5.
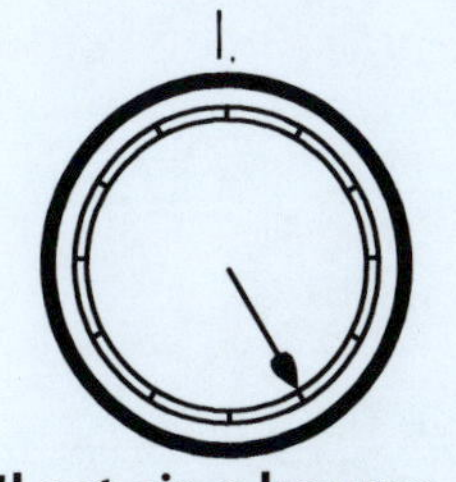	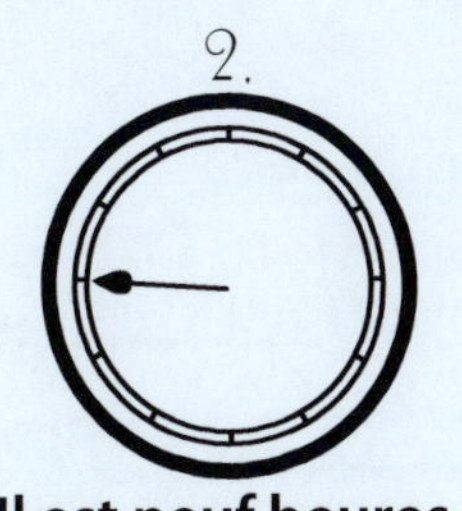	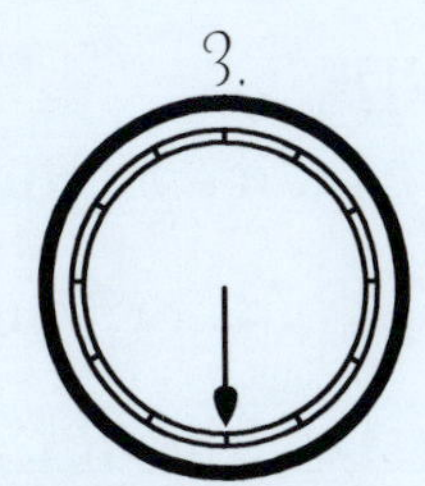	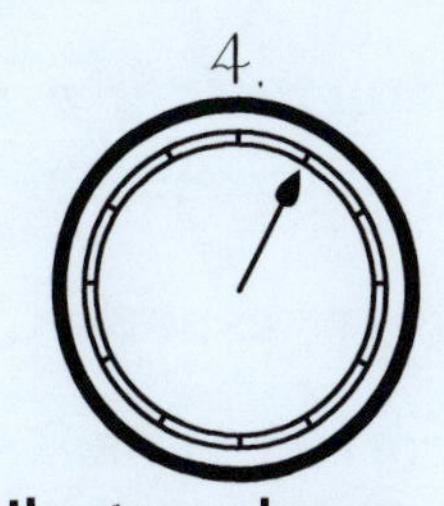	
Il est cinq heures.	Il est neuf heures.	Il est six heures.	Il est une heure.	Il est onze heures.
It is five o'clock.	It is nine o'clock.	It is six o'clock.	It is one o'clock.	It is eleven o'clock.
___	___	___	___	___

Quelle Heure Est-Il Vraiment?

Imagine you're teaching your little brother or sister how to tell time. For each clock below, you ask him/her: "**Quelle heure est-il?**" Read the different responses provided, and either say, "You're right!" (**Tu as raison!** or **Vous avez raison!** if you imagine you are teaching more than one sibling) or "You're wrong!" (**Tu as tort!** or **Vous avez tort!**). If the response is wrong, write the correct time on the line below the image of the clock face. Here is an **exemple**:

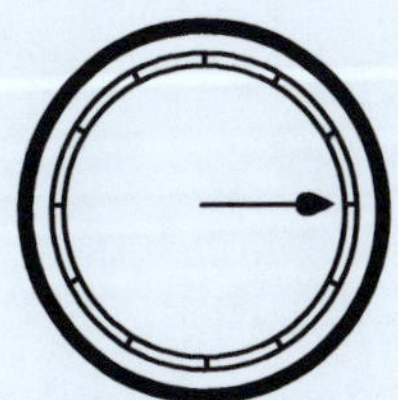

"Quelle heure est-il?"
Response: **"Hmmm . . . Il est six heures."**
Your Response: "Tu as tort!" "You're wrong!"
Correct Time: "Il est trois heures." "It is three o'clock."

1\.

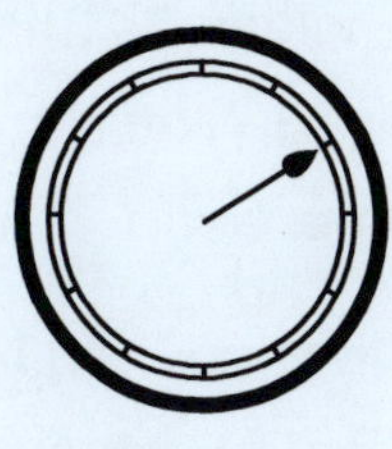

"Quelle heure est-il?"
Response: **"Il est deux heures."**
Your Response: "Tu as raison!" *or* "Vous avez raison!" "You're right!"
Correct Time: ___

2. 

"Quelle heure est-il?"
Response: "**Hmmm . . . Je ne suis pas sûr. Il est cinq heures, peut-être?**"

Your Response: **"Tu as tort!"** ***or*** **"Vous avez tort!"** "You're wrong!"

Correct Time: **"Il est dix heures."** "It is ten o'clock."

3. 

"Quelle heure est-il?"
Response: "**Je pense qu'il est trois heures.**"

Your Response: **"Tu as tort!"** ***or*** **"Vous avez tort!"** "You're wrong!"

Correct Time: **"Il est cinq heures."** "It is five o'clock."

---

4. 

"Quelle heure est-il?"
Response: "**Euh . . . il est une heure, je pense.**"

Your Response: **"Tu as raison!"** ***or*** **"Vous avez raison!"** "You're right!"

Correct Time: ____________________

---

5. 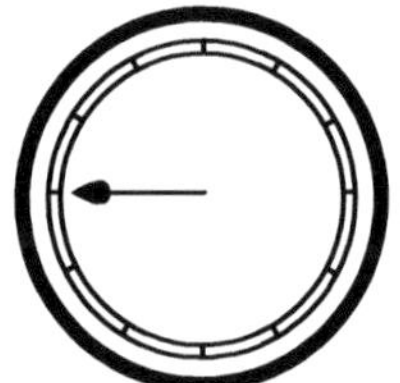

"Quelle heure est-il?"
Response: "**Il est onze heures, je suis sûr!**"

Your Response: **"Tu as tort!"** ***or*** **"Vous avez tort!"** "You're wrong!"

Correct Time: **"Il est neuf heures."** "It is nine o'clock."

Traduction

If you look back in this **chapitre**'s dialogue, you will see the question that the rabbit asks our three travelers: **"D'où est-ce que vous venez?"** (**de** + **où** + **est-ce que**). As you might have guessed from their answer (**Nous venons du village.** "We're coming from the village."), this question means, "Where are you coming from?" However, it also means, "Where do you come from?" in general, as in, what part of the world or what part of a certain country are you from?

Translate into French just the underlined questions below using your new knowledge of the verb **venir**. The beginnings of the sentences may give you clues about how to translate the sentences.

1. Those girls, where do they come from?

   Translation: **D'où est-ce qu'elles viennent?**

2. How about you guys? Where do you come from?

   Translation: **D'où est-ce que vous venez?**

3. I feel like I've seen you before at school. Where do you come from?

   Translation: **D'où est-ce que vous venez?** *or* **D'où est-ce que tu viens?**

4. He looks foreign. Where does he come from?

   Translation: **D'où est-ce qu'il vient?**

5. I've never seen so many families camp here. Where do they come from?

   Translation: **D'où est-ce qu'elles viennent?**

6. I've heard that some of our ancestors were from a different continent. Is that true?

   Where do we come from?

   Translation: **D'où est-ce que nous venons?**

TEACHER'S NOTE

In French, the word "family"—**la famille**—is feminine. Hence, since it's plural, we use **elles** with it.

GRAMMAIRE

Circle the correct answer.

1. When you ask "What time is it?" in French, you are actually asking:
   (a.) Which hour is it?
   b. Which time is it?
   c. What is the time?
   d. What is time, anyway?

2. Which of the following sentences about time is phrased *correctly*?
   a. Il est trois heure.
   b. Il est une heures.
   (c.) Il est une heure.
   d. Il est six heure.

3. What is the difference in pronunciation between the two underlined words: **Trois heures** and **Une heure**?
   (a.) There is no difference in pronunciation.
   b. You can hear a *z* sound at the end of **heures**, but not at the end of **heure**.
   c. You can hear an *s* sound at the end of **heures**, but not at the end of **heure**.
   d. The first word is pronounced *HERS* and the second is just ER.

4. Among the following possibilities, which is the only way to translate the sentence "I am right" into French?
   a. **Je suis raison.**
   b. **Je suis tort.**
   (c.) **J'ai raison.**
   d. **J'ai tort.**

Nouveau Vocabulaire

Fill in the blank with the correct translation(s) for each word.

Français	Anglais
1. **attendre, j'attends**	to wait, I wait
2. **courir, je cours**	to run, I run
3. **dormir, je dors**	to sleep, I sleep
4. **avoir raison/tort, j'ai raison/tort**	to be right/wrong, I am right/wrong
5. **venir, je viens**	to come, I come
6. **une course**	a race
7. **une cerise**	a cherry
8. **une poire**	a pear
9. **fou**	crazy
10. **vite/lent**	fast/slow

Ancien Vocabulaire

Fill in the blank with the correct translation(s) for each word.

Français	Anglais
1. **devoir, je dois**	to have to/should, I have to/should
2. **pouvoir, je peux**	to be able to, I can
3. **vouloir, je veux**	to want, I want
4. **avoir l'air (de), j'ai l'air (de)**	to seem (like), I seem (like)
5. **un berger**	a shepherd
6. **très**	very
7. **tout**	everything, all

Français	Anglais
8. **ensemble**	together
9. **une idée**	an idea
10. **un endroit**	a place

Résumé

Résumé is the French word for "summary." In this section, your job is to complete the summary of what happened in this **chapitre**'s Jean and Aurélie episode. In each sentence, there are *three* blanks. Start by completing the middle blank, which asks you for the appropriate form of the verb (you'll find the choices for the verb below the blank). After that, the verb you just chose will be *sandwiched* between two other blanks. What structure have we learned in French that *sandwiches* a verb? **Ne** and **pas**, of course! We left you two extra spaces for **ne** and **pas** because some of the sentences need to be made *negative* in order to be an accurate **résumé**, or summary, of our story!

For example:

Jean ______ est ______ **une souris.**
(**(est)** / **es** / **sont**) Jean is a mouse.

Aurélie n' est pas **une souris.**
(**(est)** / **es** / **sont**) Aurélie is not a mouse.

1. **Le lapin** ______ vient ______ **du village.**
(**(vient)** / **viens** / **venez**) The rabbit comes from the village.

2. **Il** ne court pas beaucoup.
(**cours** / **(court)** / **courons**) He doesn't run very much.

3. **Il** ______ attend ______ **la tortue.**
(**attendez** / **attends** / **(attend)**) He is waiting for the tortoise.

4. **Aurélie** ______ pense ______ **que le lapin est fou.**
(**(pense)** / **penses** / **pensent**) Aurélie thinks that the rabbit is crazy.

5. **Le lapin aime** ______ dormir ______ .
(**dort** / **dormons** / **(dormir)**) The rabbit likes to sleep.

6. **Jean, Aurélie, et Thibault** ne dorment pas **. Ils marchent.**
(**dormons** / **(dorment)** / **dormir**) Jean, Aurélie, and Thibault do not sleep.

Traduction

Translate from English to French the following sentences about different characters you've met so far in the story of Jean and Aurélie's journey.

1. The rats are making an omelet at five o'clock.

   Translation: **Les rats font une omelette à cinq heures.**

2. The wolf thinks that he looks like a shepherd. But he is wrong. He looks crazy.

   Translation: **Le loup pense qu'il a l'air d'un berger. Mais il a tort. Il a l'air fou.**

3. The guard's dog likes to sleep. He is very cute.

   Translation: **Le chien du gardien aime dormir. Il est très mignon.**

4. The rabbit wants to sleep. He does not want to run.

   Translation: **Le lapin veut dormir. Il ne veut pas courir.**

5. The turtle cannot run very fast. But the turtle doesn't sleep.

   Translation: **La tortue ne peut courir très vite. Mais la tortue ne dort pas.**

Dictée!

Listen to the audio file [08_06/Tr. 44] of the **dictée** for this **chapitre**. On the lines provided, write down the three sentences you hear. You do not need to write translations for them, though it's good practice to think through what the English translation would be. You may stop and repeat the audio file several times as you're writing down the sentences.

1. **Quelle heure est-il?**

   Translation: What time is it?

2. **Il est trois heures.**

   Translation: It is three o'clock.

3. **Non! Tu as tort!**

   Translation: No! You're wrong!

Say It Aloud!

This exercise has two parts. First, translate each sentence from English into French. Then, say each French sentence aloud, comparing your pronunciation to the audio file (09_09/Tr. 53).

1. Aurélie is eating the grapes.
   Translation: **Aurélie mange les raisins.**
2. The fox is not eating the grapes.
   Translation: **Le renard ne mange pas les raisins.**
3. "The grapes will be bad!"
   Translation: **"Les raisins vont être mauvais!"**
4. The fox is going to look for the apple trees.
   Translation: **Le renard va chercher les pommiers.**
5. "We will stay near the vines."
   Translation: **"Nous allons rester près des vignes."**
6. "You are not going to like the grapes!"
   Translation: **"Vous n'allez pas aimer les raisins!"**

Changing Tenses

Go back to the previous exercise and look only at your French translations. Rewrite the French sentences below, changing the present-tense sentences to future tense and the future-tense sentences to present tense.

1. **Aurélie va manger les raisins.**

   Aurélie is going to/will eat the grapes.

2. **Le renard ne vas pas manger de raisins.**

   The fox is not going to/will not eat the grapes.

3. **Les raisins sont mauvais.**

   The grapes are bad.

4. **Le renard cherche les pommiers.**

   The fox looks for/is looking for the apple trees.

5. Nous restons près des vignes.

   We stay/are staying close to the vines.

6. Vous n'aimez pas les raisins.

   You do not like the grapes.

I Know That You Know . . . Or Do You?

Below might be one of the most confusing sentences you've ever seen. Translate it into English on the lines provided!

Je sais que tu sais que nous savons qu'elle sait que vous savez que j'aime la grammaire.

I know that you know that we know that she knows that you know that I like grammar.

Grammaire

1. Grammatically speaking, the word "tense" means:
   (a.) time
   b. tight
   c. verb
   d. ingredient

2. Which sentence below is in the *future tense*?
   a. **Jean veut partir.** Jean wants to leave.
   b. **Le lapin ne doit pas attendre.** The rabbit should not wait.
   (c.) **Nous allons marcher.** We are going to/will walk.
   d. **Aurélie ne veut pas rester.** Aurélie does not want to stay.

3. One sentence has *one* extra word that shouldn't be there. Which sentence is it?
   a. **Vous allez courir?** Are you going to/will you run?
   (b.) **Ils vont à aimer mon gâteau.**
   c. **Thibault ne va pas rester dans le village.** Thibault is not going to/will not stay in the village.
   d. **Les chiens ne vont pas manger le chat.** The dogs are not going to/will not eat the cat.

4. Which negative sentence is *correct*?
   a. **Vous ne pas allez dormir dans la maison.**
   b. **Vous n'allez dormir pas dans la maison.**
   c. **Vous allez ne pas dormir dans la maison.**
   (d.) **Vous n'allez pas dormir dans la maison.** You are not going to/will not sleep in the house.

Nouveau Vocabulaire

Fill in the blank with the correct translation for each word.

Français	Anglais
1. **comprendre, je comprends**	to understand, I understand
2. **prendre, je prends**	to take, I take
3. **voir, je vois**	to see, I see
4. **partir, je pars**	to leave, I leave
5. **savoir, je sais**	to know, I know
6. **un raisin**	a grape
7. **une région**	a region
8. **souvent**	often
9. **le pommier**	the apple tree
10. **le cerisier**	the cherry tree
11. **la vigne**	the vine

Ancien Vocabulaire

Fill in the blank with the correct translation for each word.

Français	Anglais
1. **courir, je cours**	to run, I run
2. **une course**	a race
3. **vite/lent**	fast/slow
4. **la jambe**	the leg
5. **la main/les mains**	the hand/hands

Français	Anglais
6. **le bras**	the arm
7. **une bouche**	a mouth
8. **le pied**	the foot
9. **un œil/des yeux**	an eye/eyes
10. **le dos**	the back

The Body in Action

Draw lines to match the actions on the left with the different parts of the body used in those actions on the right.

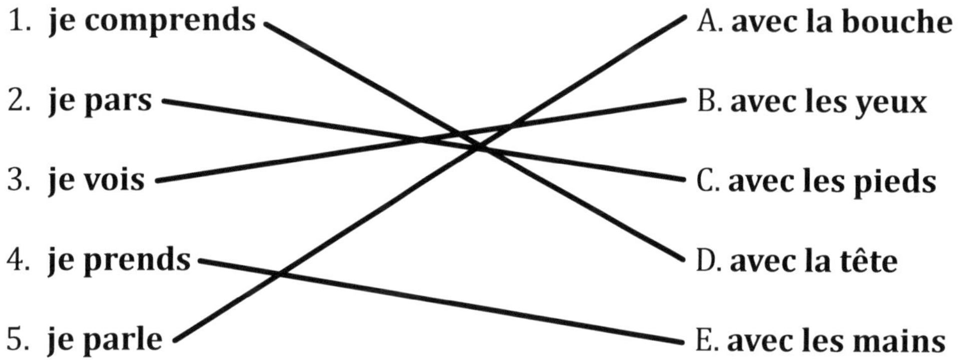

Missing Letters

In the two conjugation charts below, many of the verb forms are missing letters. Your job is to fill them in so that they're complete! We've done the first box of the first chart as an example for you.

Voir (to see)

Person	Singular	Plural
1st Person	**je v o i s** (I see)	**nous v o y o __n__ s** (we see)
2nd Person	**tu v o __i__ s** (you see)	**vous v o __y__ e z** (you see)
3rd Person	**il/elle v o i __t__** (he/she/it sees)	**ils/elles v o __i__ e n t** (they see)

Partir (to leave)

Person	Singular	Plural
1st Person	**je p a __r__ s** (I leave)	**nous p a r t __o__ n s** (we leave)
2nd Person	**tu p a __r__ s** (you leave)	**vous p a r t __e__ z** (you leave)
3rd Person	**il/elle p a r __t__** (he/she/it leaves)	**ils/elles p a r __t__ e n t** (they leave)

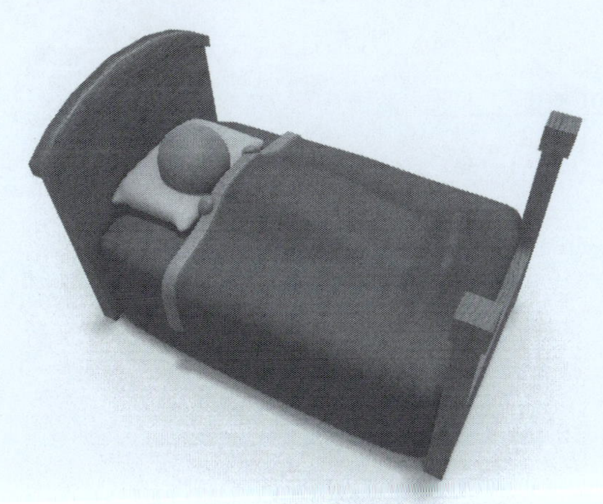

Traduction

Though the following episodes are not exactly from the dialogues of the last few **chapitres**, you will recognize the situations easily. Translate the sentences and conversations into English.

1. **Thibault, Aurélie, et Jean ne comprennent pas les rats.**
   "Est-ce que vous voyez les rats?"
   "Oui! Nous voyons les rats! Les rats prennent un œuf. Mais qu'est-ce qu'ils vont faire avec ça?!"

   Translation: Thibault, Aurélie and Jean do not understand the rats.
   "Do you see the rats?"
   "Yes, we see the rats! The rats are taking an egg. But what are they going to do with it?"

2. **Le lapin attend la tortue. Elle va arriver. Le lapin ne va pas partir avant.**
   "Pourquoi est-ce que vous partez? Vous ne voulez pas rester ici pour manger les fruits et dormir?"

   Translation: The rabbit is waiting for the turtle. She is going to arrive. The rabbit will not leave before/beforehand.
   "Why are you leaving? You do not want to stay here to eat fruit and sleep?"

3. **Le renard voit les raisins, mais il ne peut pas manger les raisins. "Je sais que ces raisins ne vont pas être délicieux!"**
   Aurélie whispers to Jean, **"Comment est-ce qu'il sait?"**
   Jean replies, **"Je ne sais pas!"**

   Translation: The fox sees the grapes, but he cannot eat the grapes. "I know that the grapes will not be delicious!"
   Aurélie whispers to Jean, "How does he know?"
   Jean replies, "I don't know!"

Dictée!

Listen to the audio file [09_10/Tr. 54] of the **dictée** for this **chapitre**. On the lines provided, write down the three sentences you hear. You do not need to write translations for them, though it's good practice to think through what the English translation would be. You may stop and repeat the audio file several times as you're writing down the sentences.

1. **Ils ne comprennent pas.**

   Translation: They don't understand.

2. **Il ne comprend pas.**

   Translation: He doesn't understand.

3. **Je vais partir.**

   Translation: I'm going to leave.

CHAPITRE 10 CINQ

In this unit, we picked up where we had left off with the special question words **qui** and **quoi**, and we added a major new verb to our list: **faire**. We then dug our heels into the *boot verbs* of **chapitre** 7 (**devoir**, **pouvoir**, **vouloir**). We followed that up with a triple whammy in **chapitre** 8: **Quelle heure est-il?** and telling time, part 6 of the Curious Haves—**avoir raison/tort**—and a whole bunch of new irregular verbs, such as **venir** and **attendre**. Finally, in **chapitre** 9, we discovered another **paquet** (bunch) of irregular verbs, as well as the *future tense* (**aller** + an infinitive verb), which lets us say "I *will* do something" or "You *are going to* do something." Take a look back over the vocabulary from the preceding four chapters and note any words with which you're still having trouble. We'll meet you on the other side for some rocking review exercises!

	French	English
☐	**faire, je fais**	to do/make, I do/make
☐	**arriver, j'arrive**	to arrive, I arrive
☐	**cacher, je cache**	to hide (something), I hide (something)
☐	**casser, je casse**	to break, I break
☐	**tirer, je tire**	to pull, I pull
☐	**dégoûtant**	disgusting
☐	**l'œuf**	the egg
☐	**l'omelette**	the omelet
☐	**le rat**	the rat
☐	**la dame**	the lady
☐	**devoir, je dois**	to have to, should; I have to, I should
☐	**pouvoir, je peux**	to be able to, I can
☐	**vouloir, je veux**	to want, I want

	French	English
☐	**cher**	expensive
☐	**si**	so
☐	**une pomme**	an apple
☐	**une fraise**	a strawberry
☐	**une pêche**	a peach
☐	**une pomme de terre**	a potato
☐	**une tomate**	a tomato
☐	**attendre, j'attends**	to wait, I wait
☐	**courir, je cours**	to run, I run
☐	**dormir, je dors**	to sleep, I sleep
☐	**avoir raison/tort, j'ai raison/tort**	to be right/wrong, I am right/wrong
☐	**venir, je viens**	to come, I come

French	English
une course	a race
une cerise	a cherry
une poire	a pear
fou	crazy
vite/lent	fast/slow
comprendre, je comprends	to understand, I understand
prendre, je prends	to take, I take
voir, je vois	to see, I see

French	English
partir, je pars	to leave, I leave
savoir, je sais	to know, I know
un raisin	a grape
une région	a region
souvent	often
le pommier	the apple tree
le cerisier	the cherry tree
une vigne	a vine

My List of Words to Master

So that you can easily review the words you are having difficulty remembering, write them down on the lines provided below.

Grammaire

The Verb *Faire* ("to do/make," Chapitre 6)

Write the correct form of the verb **faire** in the following blanks, and then translate each sentence into English.

1. **Les oiseaux** ___font___ **leurs maisons dans les arbres.**

   Translation: The birds make their houses in the trees.

2. **Son frère a cinq ans aujourd'hui. Elle** ___fait___ **un cadeau pour son anniversaire** (birthday).

   Translation: Her brother is five years old today. She is making a present/gift for his birthday.

3. **Nous avons faim! Alors, nous** ___faisons___ **un gâteau aux fraises.**

   Translation: We are hungry! So, we are making a strawberry cake.

4. **"Madame, pourquoi est-ce que vous** ___faites___ **une omelette avec des cerises!?"**

   Translation: "Madame, why are you making an omelet with cherries!?"

5. **"Ah! Ce n'est pas une omelette: je** ___fais___ **un clafoutis.[1] Quand tu** ___fais___ **un clafoutis, tu as besoin d'œufs et de cerises!"**

   Translation: "Ah! It's not an omelet: I am making a clafoutis. When you make a clafoutis, you need eggs and cherries!"

1. A **clafoutis** is a traditional French dessert. It is like a thin, spongy, cake that usually contains cherries or other fruit. Photo courtesy of Rotem Danzig, https://commons.wikimedia.org/w/index.php?curid=2354473

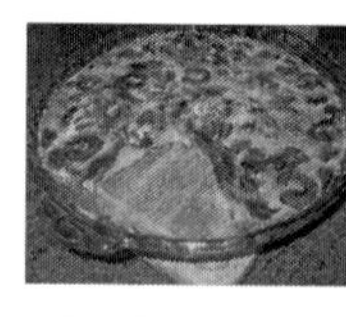

What Are They Doing?

Below there are five pictures of different people engaged in different activities. In each case, you must do two things: First, ask what the subject (in parentheses below the image) is doing by writing the question **Qu'est-ce que + faire**. Second, answer the question you formulated, still using the subject pronoun you see below the image. An example is below. By the way, to help you out with the second step, we've put the possible actions in the *infinitive* form to the right—you'll have to conjugate them, of course.

dormir	to sleep
courir	to run
jouer	to play
étudier	to study
manger	to eat

Example:

(il)

Question: **Qu'est-ce qu'il fait?** (What is he doing?)

Answer: **Il chante!** (He's singing!)

1.

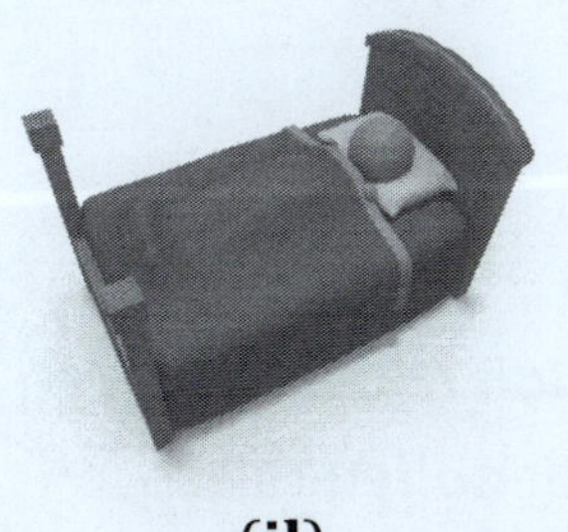

(il)

Question: **Qu'est-ce qu'il fait?**

What is he doing?

Answer: **Il dort!**

He is sleeping!

2.

(vous)

Question: **Qu'est-ce que vous faites?**

What are you doing?

Answer: **Vous étudiez!**

You are studying!

3.

(elles)

Question: **Qu'est-ce qu'elles font?**

What are they doing?

Answer: **Elle jouent!**

They are playing!

4. 

(nous)

Question: Qu'est-ce que nous faisons?

What are we doing?

Answer: Nous mangeons!

We are eating!

5. 

(il)

Question: Qu'est-ce qu'il fait?

What is he doing?

Answer: Il court!

He is running!

Boot Verbs (Chapitre 7)

Which Boot Fits?

Three of the four conjugation charts below are trying to trick you into thinking that they're the correct one for the boot verb **pouvoir**. It's your job to decide which one of the four is correct. Circle it and ignore the others once you've identified the correct one!

A.

je peut (I can)	**nous pouvons** (we can)
tu peut (you can)	**vous pouvez** (you can)
il/elle peut (he/she/it can)	**ils/elles peuvent** (they can)

B.

je peux (I can)	**nous peuvons** (we can)
tu peux (you can)	**vous peuvez** (you can)
il/elle peut (he/she/it can)	**ils/elles peuvent** (they can)

C.

je pue (I can)	**nous puons** (we can)
tu pues (you can)	**vous puez** (you can)
il/elle pue (he/she/it can)	**ils/elles puent** (they can)

(D.)

je peux (I can)	**nous pouvons** (we can)
tu peux (you can)	**vous pouvez** (you can)
il/elle peut (he/she/it can)	**ils/elles peuvent** (they can)

TEACHER'S NOTE

No! Not C! This comes from the verb **puer**, which means "to *stink*"! **Je pue** means "I stink!"

Give 'Em the Boot

Translate the following questions into French using the boot verbs you learned in **chapitre** 7. (Hint: You may recognize these situations from Jean and Aurélie's adventures.)

1. **Qu'est-ce qu'ils veulent faire avec l'œuf?**

   Translation: What do they want to do with the egg?

2. **Comment est-ce que vous pouvez trouver des fromages dans la forêt?**

   Translation: How can you find cheese in the forest?

3. **Qui veut aller à la ville?**

   Translation: Who wants to go to the city?

4. **Où est-ce que nous pouvons acheter des légumes?**

   Translation: Where can we buy vegetables?

5. **Comment est-ce que nous pouvons dormir dans la grange avec tous les animaux?**

   Translation: How can we sleep in the barn with all of the animals?

6. **Pourquoi est-ce que vous devez partir?**

   Translation: Why do you have to leave?

Telling Time, Irregular Verbs (Chapitre 8)

1. In French, how do you ask, "What time is it?"

   "Quelle heure est-il?"

2. Write down, in French, what time each clock is showing.

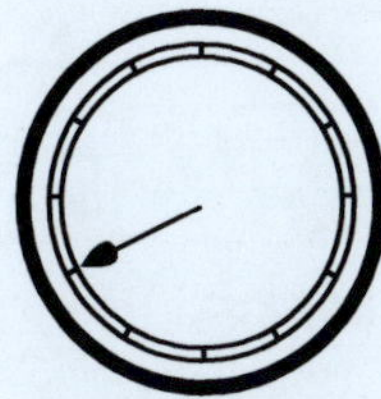

a. Il est huit heures.
It is eight o'clock

b. Il est une heure.
It is one o'clock.

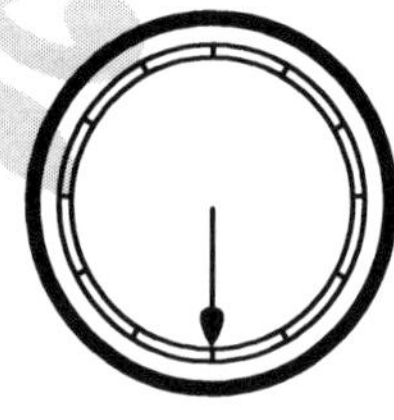

c. **Il est six heures.**

It is six o'clock.

d. **Il est midi. *or* Il est minuit. *or* Il est douze heures.**

It is noon. *or* It is midnight. *or* It is twelve o'clock.

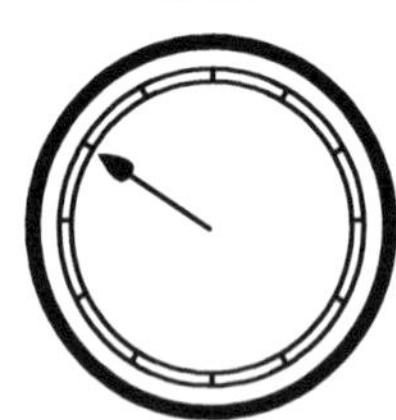

e. **Il est dix heures.**

It is ten o'clock.

3. Some Irregulars: Help sort out the confused conjugation. Cross out the incorrect verb forms and fill in the blank with the correct one. We've taken care of one box for you.

Venir (to come)

Person	Singular	Plural
1st Person	**je ~~vient~~** viens	**nous ~~viennent~~** venons
2nd Person	**tu ~~venons~~** viens	**vous ~~viennent~~** venez
3rd Person	**il/elle ~~viens~~** vient	**ils/elles ~~vient~~** viennent

4. Circle the correct conjugation of each verb.

a. **Jean et Aurélie ne ____________ pas vers la ville.**

(court / courons / courent)

Jean and Aurélie are not running toward the city.

b. **La mère de Thibault ____________ le fromage dans son village.**

(attendent / attends / attend)

Thibault's mother is waiting for the cheese in her village.

c. **Les animaux dans le zoo ____________ Jean et Aurélie.**

(attendent / attends / attend)

The animals from the zoo are waiting for Jean and Aurélie.

d. **"Nous ne _______________ pas de la forêt. Nous _______________ du zoo!"**

(viennent / (venons) / vient) (est / sont / (sommes))

"We do not come from the forest. We come from the zoo!"

e. **Thibault _______________ du village.**

((vient) / viens / viennent)

Thibault comes from the village.

f. **Le lapin ne _______________ pas. Il veut _______________ la tortue.**

(cours / courons / (court)) (attend / (attendre) / attends)

The rabbit is not running. He wants to wait for the tortoise.

The Future Tense, More Irregular Verbs (Chapitre 9)

1. **Traduction:** Translate the following conversation. If a sentence is in French, translate it into English; if it is in English, translate it into French.

A: "What are you doing?"
Translation: "Qu'est-ce que tu fais?"

B: **"J'attends mes amis."**
Translation: "I'm waiting for my friends."

A: **"Où sont tes amis?"**
Translation: "Where are your friends?"

B: "I don't know."
Translation: "Je ne sais pas."

A: **"Est-ce qu'ils vont venir?"**
Translation: "Are they going to come?"

B: "Maybe."
Translation: "Peut-être."

A: "I don't see your friends."
Translation: "Je ne vois pas tes amis."

B: **"Moi non plus."**
Translation: "Me neither."

TEACHER'S NOTE

It is also possible to translate the expression **moi non plus**—at least, in this particular dialogue, given the preceding question—as "neither do I" or "I don't either," even though that is a less literal translation.

A: "Well, then, when are you going to leave?"
Translation: "Ben, alors, quand est-ce que tu vas partir?"

B: **"Je ne sais pas."**
Translation: "I don't know."

A: "OK, well, I'm leaving now."
Translation: D'accord, ben, je pars maintenant!

B: "You're right! I'll go with you!"[2]
Translation: Tu as raison. Je vais aller avec toi!

2. **Ifs Only + Say It Aloud!** Translate the following sentences, which all begin with the word "if" (**si**). Then go back and pronounce the French sentences, comparing your pronunciation with the audio file (10_01/Tr. 55).

a. **Si tu ne manges pas, tu vas avoir faim.**
Translation: If you do not eat, you will be hungry.

b. **Si je ne cours pas, je ne vais pas arriver avant neuf heures.**
Translation: If I do not run, I will not arrive before nine o'clock.

c. **Si vous n'étudiez pas, vous n'allez pas réussir à l'école.**
Translation: If you do not study, you will not succeed at school.

d. **Si elles ne prennent pas la voiture, elles vont devoir marcher.**
Translation: If they do not take the car, they will have to walk.

e. **S'il ne voit pas ses amis au village, il va partir.**
Translation: If he does not see his friends at the village, he will leave.

2. Note: "You" = **toi** at the end of this sentence (see **chapitre** 13).

Tense

Below are several sentences from this **chapitre**'s Jean and Aurélie episode. Your job is to say whether they are in the **passé composé**, the *present tense*, or the *future tense*. Write your answers in the blanks provided.

1. **Je vois une tortue là-bas.** I see a tortoise over there.

   present tense

2. **Elle va être contente.** She is going to be/will be happy.

   future tense

3. **Vous connaissez Monsieur le lapin!?** You know Mr. Rabbit!?

   present tense

4. **Nous avons vu ton ami le lapin.** We saw your friend the rabbit.

   passé composé

5. **Nous avons commencé dimanche.** We started Sunday.

   passé composé

6. **Mais peut-être qu'il a fini de dormir!** But maybe he finished sleeping!

   passé composé

7. **Il va arriver trop tard.** He is going to/will arrive too late.

   future tense

8. **Eh ben, nous allons arriver ce soir!** Well, we are going to arrive tonight!

   future tense

Messy Calendar

Fix the calendar below by crossing out the incorrect French words for the days of the week and writing the correct ones below the English words. We've done the first one for you as an example.

Monday	Tuesday	Wednesday	Thursday	Friday	Saturday	Sunday
~~Jeudi~~	~~Lundi~~	~~Vendredi~~	~~Samedi~~	~~Dimanche~~	~~Mardi~~	~~Mercredi~~
Lundi	Mardi	Mercredi	Jeudi	Vendredi	Samedi	Dimanche

Traduction + Say It Aloud!

Translate the following sentences from French into English. Then, go back and say the French sentences aloud, comparing your pronunciation to the audio file (11_05/Tr. 60).

1. **Hier, j'ai vu ma famille.**
   Translation: Yesterday, I saw my family.

2. **Ils ont été très contents.**
   Translation: They were very happy.

3. **Ma mère a fait un gâteau.**⚜
   Translation: My mother made a cake.

4. **Je n'ai pas fait attention.**
   Translation: I did not pay attention.

5. **J'ai mangé tout le gâteau.**
   Translation: I ate all of the cake.

6. **Mon frère et mes sœurs n'ont pas aimé ça.**
   Translation: My brother and my sisters did not like that.

7. **"Qu'est-ce que tu as fait!?"**
   Translation: "What did you do!?"

8. **J'ai dû partir.**
   Translation: I had to leave.

Teacher's Note

⚜ Students have seen the word **gâteau** (cake) several times (see **chapitres** 8 and 12 of *FFCA*, for instance), but if they can't remember its translation, feel free to share it with them.

Grammaire

1. In French, the past tense is made up of:
   a. one part.
   (b.) two parts.
   c. five parts.
   d. thirty-seven-and-a-half parts, not counting subparts.

2. The verb **avoir** is an auxiliary verb when:
   a. it means "to have or to possess," as in the sentence "**J'ai un chien.**"
   b. it is used as a part of the present tense.
   (c.) it is helping form the past tense.
   d. it is used in delicate conversations.

3. To say "I didn't sing yesterday" in French, we say:
   (a.) **"Je n'ai pas chanté hier."**
   b. **"Je n'ai chanté pas hier."**
   c. **"Je n'ai chanté hier."**
   d. **"Je ne ai chanté pas hier."**

4. If a verb is regular, and ends in **-er**, the way you can figure out its past participle is by:
   a. adding an **é** to the end of the infinitive.
   (b.) replacing the **-er** of the infinitive with the ending **é**.
   c. taking off the last **r** from the infinitive.
   d. It is impossible to figure this out, since past participles are irregular.

Nouveau Vocabulaire

Fill in the blank with the correct translation for each word.

Français	Anglais
1. **connaître, je connais**	to know, I know
2. **gagner, je gagne**	to win, I win
3. **demain**	tomorrow
4. **avant**	before
5. **le soir**	the evening
6. **le matin**	the morning
7. **hier**	yesterday
8. **l'après-midi**	the afternoon
9. **la semaine**	the week
10. **tard**	late

Ancien Vocabulaire

Fill in the blank with the correct translation for each word.

Français	Anglais
1. **regarder, je regarde**	to look (at), I look (at)
2. **comprendre, je comprends**	to understand, I understand
3. **finir, je finis**	to finish, I finish
4. **travailler, je travaille**	to work, I work
5. **courir, je cours**	to run, I run
6. **trouver, je trouve**	to find, I find

Français	Anglais
7. **dormir, je dors**	to sleep, I sleep
8. **acheter, j'achète**	to buy, I buy
9. **cacher, je cache**	to hide (something), I hide (something)
10. **vouloir, je veux**	to want, I want

Jean and Aurélie's Adventures

Describe what happened on each day of this *past* week in Jean and Aurélie's lives by looking at the descriptions written in each block of the calendar. Write your description in French, using the subject(s) (underlined) and the action(s) provided (in the past tense, of course![3]). Some days have two different events. We've completed one of the descriptions for you.

Lundi
Jean et Aurélie
dormir dans la forêt
Mardi
Jean et Aurélie
parler avec Thibault
Mercredi
Thibault, Jean, Aurélie
marcher au marché avec le père de Thibault
Jeudi
Aurélie
voir le loup
Le loup
avoir faim

Vendredi
Jean, Aurélie, Thibault
trouver le village
Le gardien
être méchant
Samedi
Les rats
cacher l'œuf
Dimanche
Le lapin
commencer la course avec la tortue

Lundi: Jean et Aurélie ont dormi dans la forêt.
Jean and Aurélie slept in the forest.

Mardi: Jean et Aurélie ont parlé avec Thibault.
Jean and Aurélie spoke with Thibault.

3. Remember, if you cannot figure out what the past participle of a verb is, you can look in the conjugation charts in appendix C, or in appendix D, which covers past participles.

Mercredi: Thibault, Jean, et Aurélie ont marché au marché avec le père de Thibault.
Thibault, Jean, and Aurélie walked to the market with Thibault's father.

Jeudi: Aurélie a vu le loup. Le loup a eu faim.
Aurélie saw the wolf. The wolf was hungry.

Vendredi: Jean, Aurélie, et Thibault ont trouvé le village. Le gardien a été méchant.
Jean, Aurélie, and Thibault found the village. The guard was mean.

Samedi: Les rats ont caché l'œuf.
The rats hid the egg.

Dimanche: Le lapin a commencé la course avec la tortue.
The rabbit started the race with the turtle.

Connaître vs. Savoir

Circle the correct form of either **connaître** or **savoir**. Remember, **connaître** is used to talk about knowing things "personally" and **savoir** is used to talk about facts or abilities.

1. **Nous ne ________________ pas nager.**
   (savons / connaissons)
2. **Ah oui! Je ________________ ton père!**
   (connais / sais)
3. **Jean ________________ parler en anglais et en français.**
   (sait / connaît)
4. **Aurélie ne ________________ pas parler en anglais.**
   (connaît / sait)
5. **Le lapin ne ________________ pas où est la tortue.**
   (sait / connaît)
6. **Jean, Aurélie, et Thibault ________________ que la ville est loin.**
   (savent / connaissent)
7. **Jean et Aurélie ________________ la ville parce qu'ils ont habité là-bas.**
   (saven / connaissent)

Confused Trios

The following sentences come in groups of three, but each trio looks almost as though it's the same sentence. Translate the trio so that it's clear what the different sentences mean. We've done the first one for you as an example.

Exemple:

J'ai un chien. I have a dog.
J'ai eu un chien. I had a dog.
Je vais avoir un chien. I will have a dog.

1. **Elle veut chanter.** She wants to sing.

   Elle va chanter. She will sing.

   Elle a chanté. She sang.

2. **Ils ont une voiture.** They have a car.

   Ils vont avec la voiture. They are going with the car.

   Ils ont eu une voiture. They had a car.

3. **Il est content.** He is happy.

   Il a été content. He was happy.

   Il va être content. He will be happy.

4. **Tu veux manger le fromage.** You want to eat the cheese.

   Tu vas manger le fromage. You will eat the cheese.

   Tu as mangé le fromage. You ate the cheese.

Dictée!

Listen to the audio file [11_06/Tr. 61] of the **dictée** for this **chapitre**. On the lines provided, write down the three sentences you hear. You do not need to write translations for them, though it's good practice to think through what the English translation would be. You may stop and repeat the audio file several times as you're writing down the sentences.

1. Hier, je n'ai pas mangé. Translation: Yesterday, I didn't eat.
2. Est-ce que tu connais mon frère? Translation: Do you know my brother?
3. Ils ont vu un rat! Translation: They saw a rat!

Sentences That Just Can't Seem to Agree

In the following sentences, the past participles do not agree with the subjects. Fix the sentences by rewriting them with the correct agreement between the past participles and subjects. Then, translate each corrected sentence into English. If the subject is **je**, **tu**, **nous**, or **vous**, we have put the gender in parentheses: either masculine (m) or feminine (f).

1. **Isabelle est parti ce matin.**

   Fixed: Isabelle est partie ce matin.

   Translation: Isabelle left this morning.

2. **Nous** (m) **sommes arrivé hier. Nous** (m) **sommes venu de la ville.**

   Fixed: Nous sommes arrivés hier. Nous sommes venus de la ville.

   Translation: We arrived yesterday. We came from the village.

3. **Ils sont retourné au village.**

   Fixed: Ils sont retournés au village.

   Translation: They returned to the village.

4. **Je** (f) **suis venu à six heures.**

   Fixed: Je suis venue à six heures.

   Translation: I came at six o'clock.

5. **Jean est entrée dans le village.**

   Fixed: Jean est entré dans le village.

   Translation: Jean entered the village.

6. **Elles sont tombé de l'arbre!**

   Fixed: Elles sont tombées de l'arbre!

   Translation: They fell from the tree!

7. **Je** (m) **suis allées à la plage à dix heures.**

   Fixed: Je suis allé à la plage à dix heures.

   Translation: I went to the beach at ten o'clock.

Sniff Out the Imposters!

Remember, only the **passé composé** with **être** requires the past participle to agree with the subject. The **passé composé** with **avoir** doesn't change one bit. However, among the sentences below, several past-tense constructions with **avoir** are trying to act like the past tense with **être**. Locate these constructions and change them back by writing the corrected sentence in the blank provided. If the construction of the past tense is correct, then just write "correct" on the correction blank. Then, translate all of the sentences (the correct ones and the impostors you had to fix) into English.

1. **Finalement, nous avons trouvés le restaurant.**

   Correction: **Finalement, nous avons trouvé le restaurant.**

   Translation: **Finally, we found the restaurant.**

2. **Aurélie est partie du village.**

   Correction: **correct**

   Translation: **Aurélie left from the village.**

3. **Elles ont rencontrées un loup.**

   Correction: **Elles ont rencontré un loup.**

   Translation: **They met a wolf.**

4. **Je n'ai jamais vue le musée.**

   Correction: **Je n'ai jamais vu le musée.**

   Translation: **I never saw the museum.**

5. **Ils ont achetés trois pommes, et ensuite ils ont mangés dans les champs.**

   Correction: **Ils ont acheté trois pommes, et ensuite ils ont mangé dans les champs.**

   Translation: **They bought three apples, and then they ate in the fields.**

6. **Après le village, elles sont allées à la ville.**

   Correction: **correct**

   Translation: **After the village, they went to the city.**

Grammaire

Circle the correct answer.

1. The past tense in French can be formed with two different helping verbs: _________ and _________.
   a. **être** and **savoir**
   (b.) **avoir** and **être**
   c. **faire** and **avoir**
   d. **être** and **faire**

2. Grammatically, those two verbs are called _____________ when used to form the past tense.
   (a.) auxiliaries
   b. infinitives
   c. conjugations
   d. **passé composé**

3. What's wrong with the following sentence? **Mes chiens sont parti!** (My dogs left!)
   a. It is missing the word **ne**, because it is negative.
   b. The word **chien** should not have an **s** because it is singular.
   (c.) The word **parti** should have an **s** because it is the past participle being used with **être**.
   d. The word **sont** should be **ont** because **partir** doesn't use **être** in the **passé composé**.

4. What's wrong with the following sentence? **Je ne veux pas jamais retourner là-bas.** (I never want to go back there.)
   a. **Je** might be describing a feminine subject, so **retourner** should be **retournée**.
   b. **Là-bas** should come before **retourner**.
   c. The sentence is in the past tense, so **retourner** should be **retourné**.
   (d.) The word **jamais** (never) replaces the word **pas**, so **pas** shouldn't be in the sentence.

Nouveau Vocabulaire

Fill in the blank with the correct translation for each word.

Français	Anglais
1. **rencontrer, je rencontre**	to meet, I meet
2. **dire, je dis**	to say, I say
3. **retourner, je retourne**	to return, I return
4. **un musée**	a museum
5. **un restaurant**	a restaurant
6. **ensuite**	then, next
7. **finalement**	finally
8. **seulement**	only
9. **jamais**	never
10. **après**	after

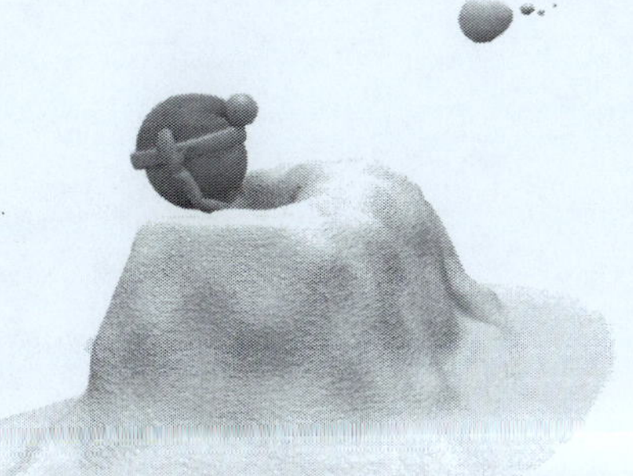

Ancien Vocabulaire

Fill in the blank with the correct translation of each word.

Français	Anglais
1. **un endroit**	a place
2. **la ferme**	the farm
3. **la grange**	the barn
4. **la montagne**	the mountain
5. **le champ**	the field
6. **le fleuve**	the river
7. **le lac**	the lake
8. **la plage**	the beach
9. **l'eau**	the water
10. **la mer**	the sea

Dites-Le À Haute Voix! (Say It Aloud!)

Fill in the following sentences using the correct form of the *past tense* of the verb indicated next to each blank in parentheses. Then, translate the sentences into English. Finally, go back and say each of the French sentences aloud, checking your answers with the audio file (12_06/Tr. 67).

1. **Hier nous** ______sommes______ ______restés______ **(rester) dans les montagnes pour seulement deux heures.**

   Translation: Yesterday we stayed in the mountains for only two hours.

2. **Elle** ______a______ ______mangé______ **(manger) mon gâteau!**

   Translation: She ate my cake!

3. **"Hé hoh! Vous** ______avez______ ______laissé______ **(laisser) vos chaussures à côté du fleuve!"**

   Translation: "Hey! You left your shoes next to the river!"

4. **À six heures aujourd'hui, je** ______suis______ ______parti______ **(partir) pour la plage.**

   Translation: At six o'clock today, I left for the beach.

5. **Hier, quand tu** (f) ______es______ ______partie______ **(partir), ils** ______ont______ ______été______ **(être) tristes.**

   Translation: Yesterday, when you left, they were sad.

TEACHER'S NOTE

Students may be tempted to write **a mangée** here. You may want to remind them that only when using the helping verb (auxiliary verb) **être** with the past tense do they need to have the participle agree with the subject.

6. **J'___ai___ ___vu___ (voir) les animaux dans la ferme. Ils ___sont venus___ (venir) près de moi.**

   Translation: I saw the animals on the farm. They came close to me.

Now try some negative sentences.

7. **Ils ___n'ont___ ___pas___ ___voulu___ (ne pas vouloir) venir au lac, alors je (ne pas aller) ___ne___ ___suis___ ___pas___ ___allé**

   Translation: They did not want to come to the lake, so I did not go.

8. **Les visiteurs ___n'ont___ ___pas___ ___pu___ (ne pas pouvoir) comprendre les enfants à l'école. Ils ___ont___ ___parlé___ (parler) trop vite.**

   Translation: The visitors were not able to/couldn't understand the kids at the school. They spoke too quickly.

9. **Je ___n'ai___ ___pas___ ___dit___ (ne pas dire) ça!**

   Translation: I didn't say that!

10. **Nous ___n'avons___ ___pas___ ___trouvé___ (ne pas trouver) notre chat.**

    Translation: We didn't find our cat.

11. **"Vous** (m) **___n'êtes___ ___jamais___ ___allés___ (ne jamais aller) aux États-Unis!?" (États-Unis** = United States).

    Translation: "You never went/have never gone to the United States!?"

He Said That She Said . . .

Figure out what happened in this ridiculous case of "whisper down the lane." Translate each step on your way down to the conclusion!

Il dit que He says that

tu dis qu'elle dit que you say that she says that

nous disons que we say that

vous dites que you say that

je dis qu'ils disent que . . . laisse tomber!

I say that they say that . . . forget it!

Dictée!

Listen to the audio file [12_07/Tr. 68] of the **dictée** for this **chapitre**. On the lines provided, write down the three sentences you hear. You do not need to write translations for them, though it's good practice to think through what the English translation would be. You may stop and repeat the audio file several times as you're writing down the sentences.

1. **Nous sommes allés à un bon restaurant.**

   Translation: We went to a good restaurant.

2. **Qu'est-ce que tu dis?**

   Translation: What are you saying?

3. **Je suis arrivé trop tard.**

   Translation: I arrived too late.

Stressed Pronouns

Je, tu, il, elle, nous, vous, ils, and **elles**—you've got these *pronouns* down pat by now. They correspond to the English words "I," "you," "he," "she," and so on. These are our *subject pronouns*, which means they can serve as the *subject*, or the "doer," of any action (verb) in a sentence. This **chapitre** introduces another set of pronouns used in different circumstances. They rarely take the place of the subject, or actor, in a sentence, but these *stressed pronouns*, as we shall see, play some pretty important roles just the same. As you read and repeat this **chapitre**'s chant, think of the following relationships between these new stressed pronouns and their English equivalents:

Person	Singular	Plural
1st Person	me à **moi**	us à **nous**
2nd Person	you à **toi**	you à **vous**
3rd Person	him à **lui** her à **elle**	them (m) à **eux** them (f) à **elles**

Renvoi

You've already seen stressed pronouns in action in this book. Check back in the Jean and Aurélie dialogues in **chapitre** 12 of *FFCA* and **chapitre** 8 of this book!

A word of caution: We cannot *always* translate our new stressed pronouns with these English words, but for the most part, they are good matchups. (We'll let you know if a translation trap is looming!) So, when do we use these guys? Here's a list of some of the instances in which they are used:

1. *When we want to give emphasis* to part of a sentence, we use a stressed pronoun (notice that in each case we stick the stressed pronoun right in front of the regular subject pronoun):

   Toi, tu es très intelligente!
   You're very smart! *or* You, you're very smart! (compared to other people)

   Lui, il connaît tous les animaux dans la forêt.
   He knows all the animals in the forest. *or* As for him, he knows all the animals in the forest. *or* This guy, he knows all the animals in the forest. (unlike other people who are not experts)

   Moi, je pense que la carte n'est pas bonne.
   I think that the map is not good. *or* Me, I think that the map is not good. *or* As for me, I think the map is not good. (Other people may trust the map, but this is my opinion).

Teacher's Note

For sentences in which the stressed pronoun is used for *emphasis*, it is not strictly necessary to translate the first, stressed pronoun. In fact, many times translating both pronouns sounds awkward in English. The essential thing is to understand that the emphasis of the sentence is on the person (or thing) designated by the two pronouns. In the answer key, we will translate sentences in the most natural way.

Pickin' Pronouns

In some of the following sentences, you will need to circle the correct pronoun to fill in the blank. In other sentences, you will need to circle whether the pronoun used in the sentence (underlined) is a stressed pronoun or a subject pronoun. In still other sentences, you'll need to do both. We've provided two examples for you.

Exemple:

Nous ne voulons pas aller au musée sans __________ (tu / (toi)).
We don't want to go to the museum without you.

Jean aime parler avec Aurélie. Il aime aussi marcher avec <u>elle</u>. ((stressed) / subject)
Jean likes to talk with Aurélie. He also likes to walk with her.

1. **Il n'a pas voulu jouer avec** __________ ((**eux**) / **ils**).
   He did not want to play with them.
2. **<u>Vous</u>, vous devez faire attention!** ((stressed) / subject)
   You should pay attention! *or* You, you should pay attention!
3. __________ (**Moi** / (**Je**)) **pense que le marché va fermer.**
   I think that the market is going to/will close.
4. **Je ne parle pas à** __________ ((**lui**) / **il**), **je parle à** __________ ((**toi**) / **tu**).
   I do not speak/am not speaking with him, I'm speaking to you.
5. __________ (**Lui** / (**Il**)) **n'est jamais retourné.**
   He never returned.
6. **Nous, <u>nous</u> savons comment aller à la ville.** (stressed / (subject))
   We know how to go to the city.
7. **Pourquoi est-ce quc tu études à côté d'<u>elle</u>? Elle parle toujours.** ((stressed) / subject)
   Why do you always study next to her? She always talks.
8. **Regarde! Les chats marchent très près de** __________ ((**moi**) / **je**).
   Look! The cats are walking very close to me.
9. __________ ((**Eux**) / **Ils**), **ils ne connaissent pas ma famille.**
   They do not know my family. *or* Those people, they do not know my family.
10. **Oh!?...** __________ ((**Tu**) / **Toi**) **as acheté un cadeau pour** __________ ((**moi**) / **je**)?
    Oh! You bought a gift for me?

Say It Aloud!

Translate the following sentences from French into English. Then, go back and say each original French sentence out loud, comparing your pronunciation to the audio file (13_05/Tr. 73).

1. **Quand est-ce que tu as parlé avec lui?**
   Translation: When did you speak with him?

2. **Toi, tu as fait un voyage magnifique!** (**faire un voyage** = go on a trip)
   Translation: You, you went on a magnificent/wonderful trip.

3. **Je vais jouer avec eux.**
   Translation: I will play with them.

4. **Est-ce que vous allez partir sans moi?**
   Translation: Are you going to leave without me?

5. **Elles, elles sont arrivées ce matin.**
   Translation: Them, they arrived this morning.

6. **Je pense que son chat a peur de toi.**
   Translation: I think that his/her cat is afraid of you.

7. **Il est méchant. Vous devez faire attention à lui.**
   Translation: He is mean. You should pay attention to him. ⚜

TEACHER'S NOTE

In French, "be careful" and "pay attention" are sometimes both expressed by the phrase **faire attention**, so in this case, we'd likely understand the second sentence in the sense of: "You should be careful with him."

Grammaire

Circle or fill in the correct answer.

1. Fix the following chart by crossing out the incorrect French translations and writing the correct translations in the blanks provided. We've done the first cell for you.

Person	Singular	Plural
1st Person	me à ~~**eux**~~ **moi**	us à **vous** nous
2nd Person	you à **moi** toi	you à **elles** vous
	him à **elle** lui	them (m) à **toi** eux
3rd Person	her à **nous** elle	them (f) à **lui** elles

2. Circle the correct answer. The chart that you just corrected shows the *only possible ways* to translate the words **moi**, **toi**, **lui**, **elle**, **nous**, **vous**, **eux**, and **elles** into English. (True / (False)) ⚜

3. A stressed pronoun, such as **moi**, **toi**, **lui**, etc., is always used after a/an:
   a. verb.
   b. adjective.
   c. conjugation.
   (d.) preposition.

TEACHER'S NOTE

For example, **mon frère et moi** translates as "my brother and *I*," not "my brother and *me*."

4. Why would you repeat the pronoun **elle** in the following sentence? **Elle, elle est intelligente.**
   (a.) to emphasize, or to underline, the idea that *she* is really smart
   b. because this sentence is actually a question
   c. because repeating the word is more polite, more formal
   d. because you're talking about two different girls, so you need two different pronouns

5. Which one of these words does not belong?
   a. **moi**
   (b.) **tu**
   c. **lui**
   d. **eux**

6. How could you say, "He and his friend know how to sing" in French?
   a. **"Il et son ami savent chanter."**
   b. **"Il et lui ami savent chanter."**
   (c.) **"Lui et son ami savent chanter."**
   d. **"Ils savent chanter."**

7. In which of the following cases would it be *incorrect* to translate **moi** as "me"?
   a. **Il ne veut pas parler avec <u>moi</u>.**
   b. **Elles ont peur de <u>moi</u>.**
   c. **Sans <u>moi</u>, vous n'allez jamais réussir.**
   (d.) **Ma sœur et <u>moi</u>, nous aimons courir dans notre maison.**

Nouveau Vocabulaire

Fill in the blank with the correct translation for each word.

Français	Anglais
1. **fermer, je ferme**	to close, I close
2. **faire une pause, je fais une pause**	to take a break, I take a break
3. **un voyage**	a trip, a voyage
4. **un magasin**	a store
5. **la route**	the road
6. **au milieu de**	in the middle of
7. **sans**	without
8. **sous**	under
9. **normal**	normal
10. **la fin**	the end

Ancien Vocabulaire

Fill in the blank with the correct translation for each word.

Français	Anglais
1. **un père**	a father
2. **une mère**	a mother
3. **un enfant**	a child
4. **un frère**	a brother
5. **une sœur**	a sister
6. **une famille**	a family
7. **une femme**	a woman, a wife

Français	Anglais
8. **un homme**	a man
9. **une fille**	a girl, a daughter
10. **un fils**	a son

Stressed Pronouns

In each of the following questions there are two sentences. The speaker really wants to make it clear about whom he is talking, so the second sentence is a repetition of the first. The second sentence contains a stressed pronoun to emphasize to *whom* he/she is referring. In the first sentence there is an underlined word, or a group of underlined words, which you must replace in the second sentence, where there is a blank. In order to do so, choose the appropriate *stressed pronoun* that would take the place of the underlined words. We've provided an example:

Exemple:

J'ai peur de Pierre. J'ai peur de lui. I'm afraid of Pierre. I'm afraid of him.

1. **La tortue a fait une course avec son ami. Elle a fait une course avec** lui
   The tortoise had a race with her friend. She had a race with him.
2. **Aurélie marche avec Thibault et Jean. Elle marche à côté d'** eux**.**
   Aurélie is walking/walks with Thibault and Jean. She is walking/walks next to them.
3. **Les rats ont eu peur du renard. Ils ont eu peur de** lui**.**
   The rats are afraid. They are afraid of him.
4. *Aurélie explains,* **"Thibault veut venir à la ville avec Jean et moi. Thibault veut venir avec** nous**."** Aurélie explains, "Thibault wants to come to the city with Jean and me. Thibault wants to come with us."
5. **Thibault pense beaucoup à sa mère et à ses sœurs. Il pense beaucoup à** elles**.**
   Thibault thinks a lot about his mother and about his sisters. He thinks a lot about them.
6. *Thibault thinks,* **"Je vais acheter du fromage pour ma mère. Je vais acheter du fromage pour** elle**."** Thibault thinks, "I am going to/I will buy cheese for my mother. I am going to/will buy cheese for her."

Teacher's Note

Tortue (tortoise/turtle) isn't one of the vocabulary words in this book, but students have seen it several times before (see **chapitres** 8 and 11, for example). However, if they can't remember the translation, feel free to share it with them.

A more natural translation of sentence 5 would be to say, "He thinks often of them."

Emphasis with Stressed Pronouns + Say It Aloud!

Make the sentences below a little bit stronger by adding the correct stressed pronoun at the beginning. Follow the provided example. Then, translate the sentences into English. Finally, go back and say the sentences aloud, comparing your pronunciation to the audio file (13_06/Tr. 74).

Exemple:

Nous, nous savons faire des bons gâteaux.
Translation: **We know how to make good cakes.**

1. Eux, **ils veulent aller à la plage.**

   Translation: They want to go to the beach.

2. Vous, **vous comprenez?**

   Translation: You understand? *or* Do you understand?

3. Elle, **elle ne sait pas parler français.**

   Translation: She does not know how to speak French.

4. Lui, **il n'a pas pu venir à ma fête (fête =** party**) d'anniversaire (anniversaire** = birthday).

   Translation: He could not come to my birthday party.

5. Moi, **je dois faire mes devoirs.**

   Translation: I have to do my homework.

6. Toi, **tu es tombée de l'arbre?**

   Translation: You fell from the tree?

7. Elles, **elles sont très gentilles.**

   Translation: They are very nice.

8. Nous, **nous sommes arrivés à sept heures.**

   Translation: We arrived at seven o'clock.

Q

Dictée!

Listen to the audio file [13_07/Tr. 75] of the **dictée** for this **chapitre**. On the lines provided, write down the three sentences you hear. You do not need to write translations for them, though it's good practice to think through what the English translation would be. You may stop and repeat the audio file several times as you're writing down the sentences.

1. **Je suis d'accord avec lui.**

   Translation: I agree with him.

2. **Nous avons peur d'elle.**

   Translation: We are afraid of her.

3. **Je veux parler avec eux.**

   Translation: I want to speak with them.

Pronominal Verbs

In this **chapitre** we're tackling a new type of verb, one that uses a little "helper word" that comes before it. These verbs are called *pronominal verbs* ("pronominal" simply means "related to pronouns"). So, how do these verbs work, and what do pronouns have to do with them? Well, it turns out that the little helper word is itself a type of pronoun, but not a type that we've seen before. Let's take a closer look at how they work with two examples, one from the chant and the other from the Conversation Journal. Pay particular attention to the underlined words:

se lever

Person	Singular	Plural
1st Person	**je me lève** (I get up)	**nous nous levons** (we get up)
2nd Person	**tu te lèves** (you get up)	**vous vous levez** (you get up)
3rd Person	**il/elle se lève** (he/she/it gets up)	**ils/elles se lèvent** (they get up)

s'appeler

Person	Singular	Plural
1st Person	**je m'appelle** (My name is)	**nous nous appelons** (our name is)
2nd Person	**tu t'appelles** (Your name is)	**vous vous appelez** (your name is)
3rd Person	**il/elle s'appelle** (His/her/its name is)	**ils/elles s'appellent** (their name is)

The underlined words (that is, the helpers) are called *reflexive pronouns*. Here they are in a table:

Person	Singular	Plural
1st Person	**me**	**nous**
2nd Person	**te**	**vous**
3rd Person	**se**	**se**

As you look back at the chant (**se lever**), you'll notice that apart from these reflexive pronouns joining the verb forms, there is nothing else that changes about the way we conjugate the verb. In this case **lever** is a regular old **-er** verb, with the same conjugations we're used to (including the **accent grave** ` that occurs in the "boot" pattern).

Teacher's Note

As indicated in the Conversation Journal, **Je m'appelle** could equally be translated "I am called" (as with the other forms: "you are called, he is called," etc.)

Swing Your (Pronominal) Partner Round and Round

Because one key to using pronominal verbs is getting the right pairing between the subject pronoun and the reflexive pronoun, we need practice in matching these "pronominal partners" together. In this exercise, draw a line that matches the subject to the correct reflexive pronoun. Remember that a certain reflexive pronoun will be used (much) more than once!

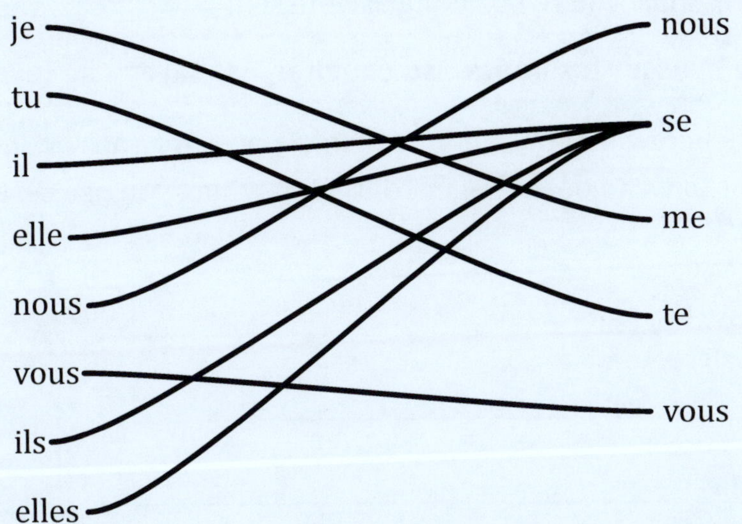

Once you're finished, write out the pairings here, and practice saying each pair aloud a few times:

je **me**

tu **te**

il **se**

elle **se**

nous **nous**

vous **vous**

ils **se**

elles **se**

Night and Day

Using five verbs from our **vocabulaire** section (see the box below), describe your night-time, and then your morning routine in chronological order. We've provided the words **d'abord**, "first"; **ensuite**, "next"; and **finalement**, "finally". There is not a single "right" answer in terms of the order in which you do things (and, of course, we've left out a lot of other steps you take since we're only using five verbs!). You should use the first person singular pronoun **je** ("I") here, since you're speaking as yourself.

s'habiller   se brosser les dents   se coucher   se laver   se lever

We've provided a guide below that has enough blank spaces for each action to be used once. However, if you want to write out a longer routine in which you use certain verbs more than once, feel free!

TEACHER'S NOTE

Answers may vary here with respect to order. However, the verb forms should match those indicated in the answer key.

D'abord je me brosse les dents,
First, I brush my teeth,

ensuite je me lave,
then, I wash up,

ensuite je me couche,
then, I go to bed,

ensuite je me lève,
then, I wake up,

et finalement je m'habille.
finally, I get dressed.

Traduction + Say it Aloud!

Translate the following sentences from French into English. Then, go back and say the French sentences aloud, comparing your pronunciation to the audio file [14_05/Tr. 80].

1. **Jean et Thibault vont se coucher avec les vaches.**

   Translation: Jean and Thibault will sleep with the cows.

2. **Mme la Tortue se lève tôt; le lapin se lève tard.**

   Translation: Madame Tortoise gets up early; the rabbit gets up late.

3. **Nous nous brossons les dents à neuf heures.**

   Translation: We brush our teeth at nine o'clock.

4. **Nous ne nous brossons pas les dents à trois heures!**[1]

Translation: **We do not brush our teeth at three o'clock!**

5. **Est-ce que tu te promènes dans la forêt?**

Translation: **Do you go for walks in the forest?**

6. **Non, je ne me promène pas dans la forêt. Les endroits intéressants se trouvent dans la ville!**

Translation: **No, I do not go for walks in the forest. The interesting places are located in the city!** ⚜

TEACHER'S NOTE

A more natural translation for the second sentence might be: "The interesting places are in the city," which means basically the same thing.

Grammaire

1. Which list contains just the *reflexive* pronouns in French?

   a. **je, me, tu, te, il, se, elle, se, nous, nous, vous, vous, ils, se, elles, se**
   b. **je, tu, il, elle, nous, vous, ils, elles**
   c. **moi, toi, lui, elle, nous, vous, eux, elles**
   (d.) **me, te, se, nous, vous, se**

2. What does it mean that certain pronominal verbs are *reciprocal*?

   a. These verbs express actions that subjects want to do.
   (b.) These verbs express actions that two subjects are doing to each other or for each other.
   c. These verbs express actions that reflect back on or affect their subjects.
   d. These verbs express actions that are illegal.

3. Is there anything special about the *infinitive* forms of pronominal verbs?

   a. No.
   b. Yes. They all end in **-er**.
   c. Yes. They are always used with the reflexive pronoun **se**.
   (d.) Yes. They are always used with a reflexive pronoun that matches the subject.

4. What difference is there in the ways to say "there is" and "there are" in French?

   a. We use the expression **il y a** for "there is" and **il y ont** for "there are."
   (b.) There is no difference: Both ideas can be expressed by saying **il y a**.
   c. We do not have any way to say these things in French.
   d. We use **ils ont** for "there are" and **il a** for "there is."

1. Did you see where we put the little negative word **ne**? It comes in between the subject (in this case **nous**) and the reflexive pronoun (also **nous** here). The **ne . . . pas** structure still applies to pronominal verbs!

Nouveau Vocabulaire

Fill in the blank with the correct translation for each word.

Français	Anglais
1. **s'habiller, je m'habille**	to get dressed, I get dressed
2. **se brosser (les dents), je me brosse (les dents)**	to brush (your teeth), I brush (my teeth)
3. **se coucher, je me couche**	to go to bed, I go to bed
4. **se laver, je me lave**	to wash (oneself), I wash myself
5. **se lever, je me lève**	to get up, I get up
6. **se promener, je me promène**	to go for a walk, I go for a walk
7. **se trouver, je me trouve**	to be located, I am located
8. **même**	same
9. **quelque chose**	something/anything
10. **il y a**	there is/there are
11. **une dent**	a tooth

Ancien Vocabulaire

Fill in the blank with the correct translation for each word.

Français	Anglais
1. **magnifique**	magnificent
2. **délicieux**	delicious
3. **facile**	easy
4. **sympathique (sympa)/gentil**	nice
5. **méchant**	mean

Français	Anglais
6. **amusant**	funny
7. **moche**	ugly
8. **heureux**	happy
9. **bizarre**	bizarre
10. **mignon**	cute

I Wash My Hands of It!

Here is a chart of the verb **se laver** (to wash up), which can also be used in the same way as **se brosser (les dents)**. That is, you can say **se laver les cheveux** (to wash one's hair) or **se laver les mains** (to wash one's hands). Complete the following chart using your new knowledge of pronominal verbs; the English translations are provided.

Se laver les mains (to wash one's hands)

Person	Singular	Plural
1st Person	**Je me lave les mains.** (I wash my hands.)	**Nous nous lavons les mains.** (We wash our hands.)
2nd Person	**Tu te laves les mains.** (You wash your hands.)	**Vous vous lavez les mains.** (You wash your hands.)
3rd Person	**Il se lave les mains. Elle se lave les mains.** (He washes his hands. She washes her hands.)	**Ils se lavent les mains. Elles se lavent les mains.** (They wash their hands.)

Q

Question Formation

For each of the following statements, think of a *question* (**une question**—abbreviated as **Q**) that could have prompted that statement as an answer (in French, a **réponse**—abbreviated as **R**). Here are the steps you should take:

1. On the line provided, translate the **réponse** into English.
2. Come up with a good question that would produce that answer.
3. Write the question in French on the line provided.
4. Translate your French question into English on the line provided.

Before you start, check out the following example:

Q: Pourquoi est-ce que tu te laves les mains?
Translation: Why are you washing your hands?

R: Je me lave les mains parce que j'ai joué avec les cochons!
Translation: I'm washing my hands because I played with the pigs!

1. **Q:** Quand est-ce qu'ils se brossent les dents?

   Translation: When do they brush their teeth?

   R: Ils se brossent les dents à neuf heures.

   Translation: They brush their teeth at nine o'clock.

TEACHER'S NOTE
À quelle heure would also be correct here.

2. **Q:** Où est-ce que tu t'habilles?

   Translation: Where do you get dressed?

   R: Je m'habille dans ma chambre. (**une chambre** = a bedroom)

   Translation: I get dressed in my bedroom.

3. **Q:** Où est-ce qu'elles se lavent les mains?

   Translation: Where do they wash their hands?

   R: Elles se lavent les mains dans la salle de bain. (**une salle de bain** = a bathroom)

   Translation: They wash their hands in the bathroom.

4. **Q:** Quand est-ce que vous vous levez?

Translation: When do you wake up?

R: Nous nous levons tôt le matin. (**tôt le matin** = early in the morning)

Translation: We wake up early in the morning.

5. **Q:** Pourquoi est-ce qu'ils se couchent tard?

Translation: Why are they going to bed late?

R: Ils se couchent tard parce qu'ils ne sont pas fatigués!

Translation: They're going to bed late because they are not tired!

Dictée!

Listen to the audio file [14_06/Tr. 81] of the **dictée** for this **chapitre**. On the lines provided, write down the three sentences you hear. You do not need to write translations for them, though it's good practice to think through what the English translation would be. You may stop and repeat the audio file several times as you're writing down the sentences.

1. Il veut se promener.

   Translation: He wants to go for a walk.

2. Est-ce que tu as envie de te promener?

   Translation: Do you feel like going for a walk?

3. Je me brosse les dents, et ensuite je me brosse les cheveux!

   Translation: I brush my teeth, and then (or next) I brush my hair!

Être, the Multitasker

Do you know what a multitasker is? It's someone who can do many things at once. Well, the verb **être** is a bit of a multitasker, as you may have noticed in your study of French. It can function as its own verb (the verb "to be"), or it can help form the past tense—**le passé composé**—for both pronominal and non-pronominal verbs. In the following sentences, identify whether **être** is being used as its *own verb*, with a *pronominal verb*, or with a *non-pronominal* (normal) verb. In the blanks provided next to the word "code," you can identify these sentences as *O* (own verb), *PP* (pronominal past), or *NP* (normal past). (These are not official codes, of course—they're just to help us practice.) Then, translate the sentences. Here are a couple of examples:

Example 1: **Les pêches sont chères ici!**
Code: O
Translation: The peaches are expensive here.

Example 2: **Les rats se sont inquiétés du renard.**
Code: PP
Translation: The rats worried about the fox.

1. **Les fromages sont délicieux.**
   Code: O
   Translation: The cheeses are delicious.

2. **Le lapin (rabbit) ne s'est pas dêpéché dans sa course avec la tortue (turtle/tortoise).**
   Code: PP
   Translation: The rabbit did not hurry in his race with the turtle.

3. **Nous nous sommes endormis dans la voiture.**
   Code: PP
   Translation: We fell asleep in the car.

4. **Thibault est retourné à la campagne avec ses fromages.**
   Code: NP

   Translation: Thibault returned to the countryside with his cheeses.

5. **La mère de Thibault ne s'est pas inquiétée pendant** (**pendant** = during) **son voyage.**
   Code: PP

   Translation: Thibault's mother did not worry during his trip.

6. **Il est d'accord avec moi.** (Hint: Check out the vocabulary from **chapitre** 4!)
   Code: O

   Translation: He agrees with me.

7. **Ils sont arrivés au marché dans l'après-midi.**
   Code: NP

   Translation: They arrived at the market in the afternoon.

The Anti-Dialogue

Let's see what would happen if we made some of the positive sentences from this week's dialogue into *negative* sentences. To do this, first add your **ne . . . pas . . .** sandwich to the correct place in the sentence. Then, translate the sentences. Check out the following example before you get started:

Example: AURÉLIE. **Nous ^ne devons ^pas nous dépêcher si nous voulons acheter les fromages.**

Translation: We must not hurry if we want to buy the cheese.

1. JEAN. **Aurélie ^n' a ^pas raison!**

   Translation: **Aurélie is not right!**

2. THIBAULT. **Pourquoi est-ce que vous ^ne vous inquiétez ^pas ?**

   Translation: **Why aren't you worrying?**

3. **Je ^ne me suis ^pas occupé de ça!**

   Translation: **I did not take care of that!**

4. **Je ^ne me suis ^pas souvenu!** (Hint: The word **souvenu** is the past participle of a verb in this **chapitre**'s **vocabulaire**. I'll bet you can guess which one!)

   Translation: **I did not remember!**

5. AURÉLIE. **Oh purée, il ^n' est ^pas très fort, Thibault!**

   Translation: **Holy smokes, he is not very good, Thibault!** *or* **Holy smokes, he is not very capable, Thibault!**

TEACHER'S NOTE

This sentence could technically be translated "Thibault's mother did not worry during *her* trip," but from the context, it makes more sense to use the translation provided here.

L'éditeur est en vacances! (The editor is on vacation!)

The tireless editor of *French for Children Primer B* finally decided enough was enough and took a small vacation as we were writing this book. While he was away, several sentences suffered various kinds of grammatical and vocabulary-related difficulties. Using the English sentences as a guide, fix the French sentences so that they are correct. Write each corrected French sentence on the line provided. Sometimes the mistake is a wrong word and sometimes the mistake has to do with the pronominal verb. Several sentences have multiple mistakes!

1. Incorrect: **Les animaux dans le zoo se couche tard.**
   English: The animals in the zoo go to bed late.

   Correct: Les animaux dans le zoo se couchent tard.

2. Incorrect: **Le village se trouvent dans la ville.**
   English: The village is located in the countryside.

   Correct: Le village se trouve dans la campagne.

3. Incorrect: **Le loup s'êtes dépêché pour aller aux champs.**
   English: The wolf hurried to go to the fields.

   Correct: Le loup s'est dépêché pour aller aux champs.

4. Incorrect: **Nous ne nous sommes endormis pas à l'école!**
   English: We did not fall asleep at school!

   Correct: Nous ne nous sommes pas endormis à l'école!

5. Incorrect: **Je veux se coucher tôt ce matin.**
   English: I want to go to bed early this evening.

   Correct: Je veux me coucher tôt ce soir.

6. Incorrect: **Est-ce que vous voulez se promener?**
   English: Do you want to go for a walk?

   Correct: Est-ce que vous voulez vous promener?

7. Incorrect: **Les amis ne se sommes pas parlé.**
   English: The friends did not talk to each other.

   Correct: Les amis ne se sont pas parlé.

Grammaire

1. Which of the following verbs use some form of **être** as a helping verb in the past tense? Circle each verb.
   - (a.) **aller**
   - (b.) **venir**
   - (c.) **se souvenir**
   - d. **manger**
   - (e.) **s'inquiéter**
   - f. **vouloir**

2. How would you translate the words **se sont** in the following sentence: **"Les souris se sont amusées"**?
   - (a.) Trick question! You cannot directly translate **se sont**: the word **se** is a part of the pronominal verb **s'amuser** (to have fun) and the word **sont** is just a helping verb making the sentence past tense. The sentence should be translated simply as, "The mice had fun."
   - b. The word **se** means "himself" and **sont** means "are," so the correct translation of the sentence is "The mice himself are fun."
   - c. The word **se** means "themselves" and **sont** means "are," so the correct translation of the sentence is, "The mice themselves are fun."
   - d. The word **se** means "each other" and **sont** means "are," so the correct translation of the sentence is, "The mice are fun with each other."
3. Which of the following is the correct French translation of the sentence "I will not go to bed!"?
   - a. **"Je ne vais se coucher pas!"**
   - b. **"Je ne vais me coucher pas!"**
   - c. **"Je ne vais pas se coucher!"**
   - (d.) **"Je ne vais pas me coucher!"**
4. Which of the following is the correct French translation of the sentence: "He took care of his cat"?
   - a. **"Il est occupé de son chat."**
   - b. **"Il s'occupe est de son chat."**
   - (c.) **"Il s'est occupé de son chat."**
   - d. **"Ill s'occuper de son chat."**

Nouveau Vocabulaire

Fill in the blank with the correct translation for each word.

Français	Anglais
1. **s'amuser, je m'amuse**	to have fun, I have fun
2. **se dépêcher, je me dépêche**	to hurry, I hurry
3. **s'endormir, je m'endors**	to fall asleep, I fall asleep
4. **s'inquiéter (de), je m'inquiète (de)**	to worry about, I worry about
5. **s'occuper de, je m'occupe de**	to take care of, I take care of
6. **se sentir, je me sens**	to feel, I feel
7. **se souvenir (de), je me souviens (de)**	to remember (**de** + something), I remember (**de** + something)
8. **fort**	strong
9. **la campagne**	the countryside
10. **mieux**	better

Teacher's Note

As noted in the vocabulary list, **fort** can also mean "good" or "capable" as a more familiar, colloquial expression.

Ancien Vocabulaire

Fill in the blank with the correct translation for each word.

Français	Anglais
1. **faire une pause, je fais une pause**	to take a break, I take a break
2. **le soir**	the evening
3. **le matin**	the morning
4. **hier**	yesterday
5. **l'après-midi**	the afternoon

Français	Anglais
6. **la semaine**	the week
7. **demain**	tomorrow
8. **tard**	late
9. **quelque chose**	something/anything
10. **il y a**	there is/there are

Back to the Future

The following sentences are in the present tense. Your job is to:

a. **Say it Aloud!** Practice reading the sentence out loud, and compare your version to the audio file/track [15_05/Tr. 86].
b. Translate the sentence into English.
c. Change the sentence so that it is in either the future tense or the past tense. Out of the six sentences, choose three for the future tense and three for the past tense (it doesn't matter which three you choose for which tense).

1. **Je me brosse les dents très tôt le matin.**

Translation: **I brush my teeth very early in the morning.**

Change Tense: **Past: Je me suis brossé les dents très tôt le matin.**

Future: Je vais me brosser les dents très tôt le matin.

2. **Vous vous amusez au musée!**

Translation: **You are having fun at the museum!**

Change Tense: **Past: Vous vous êtes amusés au musée!**

Future: Vous allez vous amuser au musée!

3. **Aurélie ne se souvient pas de comment aller au marché.**

   Translation: Aurélie does not remember how to go to the market.

   Change Tense: Past: Aurélie ne s'est pas souvenue de comment aller au marché.

   Future: Aurélie ne va pas se souvenir de comment aller au marché.

4. **Je me sens bien au milieu de la forêt.**

   Translation: I feel good in the middle of the forest.

   Change Tense: Past: Je me suis senti bien au milieu de la forêt.

   Future: Je vais me sentir bien au milieu de la forêt.

5. **Les moutons s'inquiètent du nouveau berger.**

   Translation: The sheep are worried about the new shepherd.

   Change Tense: Past: Les moutons se sont inquiétés du nouveau berger.

   Future: Les moutons vont s'inquiéter du nouveau berger.

6. **Les garçons ne se regardent pas.**

   Translation: The boys are not looking at each other.

   Change Tense: Past: Les garçons ne se sont pas regardés.

   Future: Les garçons ne vont pas se regarder.

Dictée!

Listen to the audio file [15_06/Tr. 87] of the **dictée** for this **chapitre**. On the lines provided, write down the three sentences you hear. You do not need to write translations for them, though it's good practice to think through what the English translation would be. You may stop and repeat the audio file several times as you're writing down the sentences.

1. **Ils vont se laver les mains.**

   Translation: They will wash their hands.

2. **Nous n'allons pas nous brosser les dents.**

   Translation: We will not brush our teeth.

3. **Elle s'est couchée tard.**

   Translation: She went to bed late.

CHAPITRE 16 SEIZE

It's time for a quick review of **chapitres** 11–15. In this **partie**, you learned about the past tense, or **passé composé**, starting in **chapitre** 11, where you saw how to form it with **avoir**. In **chapitre** 12, you learned that the verb **être** is sometimes—though not often—used to make the **passé composé**, too. Finally, in **chapitre** 13, you discovered the difference between *stressed pronouns* such as **moi**, **toi**, **lui**, etc., and the regular old *subject pronouns* you're used to: **je**, **tu**, **il**, **elle**, **nous**, etc.

Let's begin with a review of the vocabulary. Then, it's on to the review exercises!

	French	English
☐	**connaître, je connais**	to know, I know
☐	**gagner, je gagne**	to win, I win
☐	**demain**	tomorrow
☐	**avant**	before
☐	**le soir**	the evening
☐	**le matin**	the morning
☐	**hier**	yesterday
☐	**l'après-midi**	the afternoon
☐	**la semaine**	the week
☐	**tard**	late
☐	**rencontrer, je rencontre**	to meet, I meet
☐	**dire, je dis**	to say, I say
☐	**retourner, je retourne**	to return, I return
☐	**un musée**	a museum

	French	English
☐	**un restaurant**	a restaurant
☐	**ensuite**	then/next
☐	**finalement**	finally
☐	**seulement**	only
☐	**jamais**	never
☐	**après**	after
☐	**fermer, je ferme**	to close, I close
☐	**faire un pause, je fais une pause**	to take a break, I take a break
☐	**un voyage**	a trip, voyage
☐	**un magasin**	a store
☐	**la route**	the road
☐	**au milieu de**	in the middle of
☐	**sans**	without
☐	**sous**	under

French	English
☐ normal(e)	normal
☐ la fin	the end
☐ s'habiller, je m'habille	to get dressed, I get dressed
☐ se brosser (les dents), je me brosse (les dents)	to brush (your teeth), I brush (my teeth)
☐ se coucher, je me couche	to go to bed, I go to bed
☐ se laver, je me lave	to wash (oneself), I wash myself
☐ se lever, je me lève	to get up, I get up
☐ se promener, je me promène	to go for a walk, I go for a walk
☐ se trouver, je me trouve	to be located, I am located
☐ même	same
☐ quelque chose	something/anything
☐ il y a	there is/there are

French	English
☐ s'amuser, je m'amuse	to have fun, I have fun
☐ se dépêcher, je me dépêche	to hurry, I hurry
☐ s'endormir, je m'endors	to fall asleep, I fall asleep
☐ s'inquiéter (de/pour), je m'inquiète (de/pour)	to worry about, I worry about
☐ s'occuper de, je m'occupe de	to take care of, I take care of
☐ se sentir, je me sens	to feel, I feel
☐ se souvenir (de), je me souviens (de)	to remember (**de** + something), I remember (**de** + something)
☐ fort	strong, good, capable
☐ la campagne	the countryside
☐ mieux	better

GRAMMAIRE

The *Passé Composé* with *Avoir* (Chapitre 11)

Circle or fill in the correct answers.

1. What is wrong with all of the following sentences, which use the **passé composé**?
   Nous avons chante aujourd'hui.
   Vous n'avez pas mange vos cerises!
   J'ai rencontre un loup à côté de la route.
   Finalement, elle a gagne la course.

   a. The past participles of the sentences do not agree with the subjects. For example, **Nous avons chante** should be **Nous avons chantes**.

   b. These verbs need to use **être** to form the **passé composé**.

   (c.) The past participles do not have any accents on the final **e**.

   d. These sentences are actually in the future tense.

2. What is wrong with all of the following sentences, which use the **passé composé**?
   Ils ont cachés leur œuf sous l'arbre.
   Elles n'ont pas cassées la voiture.
   Elle a tirée son chat par la queue.
   Vous avez travaillés seulement sept heures?

   a. The forms of **avoir** are not correct.

   (b.) The past participles agree with the subjects, but they should not, since the helping verb is **avoir**, not **être**.

   c. There are too many accents on the past participles.

   d. You shouldn't use the **passé composé** unless you are a trained specialist.

3. Now that you've determined what's wrong with the sentences in the two previous exercises, correct the sentences and then translate them into English.

   a. **Nous avons chante aujourd'hui.**

   Correction: Nous avons chanté aujourd'hui.

   Translation: We sang today.

b. **Vous n'avez pas mange vos cerises!**

Correction: Vous n'avez pas mangé vos cerises!

Translation: You didn't eat your cherries!

c. **J'ai rencontre un loup à côté de la route.**

Correction: J'ai rencontré un loup à côté de la route.

Translation: I met a wolf next to the road.

d. **Finalement, elle a gagne la course.**

Correction: Finalement, elle a gagné la course.

Translation: Finally, she won the race.

e. **Ils ont cachés leur œuf sous l'arbre.**

Correction: Ils ont caché leur œuf sous l'arbre.

Translation: They hid their egg beneath the tree.

f. **Elles n'ont pas cassées mon nez.**

Correction: Elles n'ont pas cassé mon nez.

Translation: They did not break my nose.

g. **Elle a tirée son chat par la queue.**

Correction: Elle a tiré son chat par la queue.

Translation: She pulled her cat by the tail.

h. **Vous avez travaillés seulement sept heures?**

Correction: Vous avez travaillé seulement sept heures?

Translation: You worked for only seven hours?

The *Passé Composé* with *Être* (Chapitre 12)

1. Some verbs use **avoir** to form the **passé composé**, or past tense, while other verbs use **être**. When used as helping (auxiliary) verbs, we call **avoir** and **être**:

   a. infinitives.
   b. conjugations.
   c. irregular verbs.
   (d.) auxiliary verbs.

2. Why does the word **retournées** end in **e** and an **s** in the following sentence? **Les filles sont retournées!** The girls returned!

   a. If the past participle is used with **être**, it always receives extra letters.
   (b.) If the **passé composé** is formed with **être**, the past participle needs to agree with the subject.
   c. **Les filles** always requires an extra **e** and **s** in the past participle, no matter if it's with **avoir** or with **être**. For example: **Les filles ont chantées.**
   d. The author of this book must have been half asleep while writing that sentence.

3. One common feature of verbs that use **être** to form the **passé composé** is that:

   (a.) They are often verbs describing *movement.*
   b. They are usually verbs with *three or more syllables.*
   c. They are always *irregular verbs.*
   d. The past participles of these verbs *always have an extra **e**.*

4. The verbs in the following box are all mixed up. Some of them use **avoir** to form the past tense (**passé composé**), but others use **être**. Your job is to assign each verb to the correct list beneath the box. We've done one as an example for you.

aller	~~**manger**~~	**tomber**
travailler	**partir**	**acheter**
casser	**étudier**	**entrer**
parler	**pouvoir**	**devoir**
rester	**vouloir**	**réussir**
retourner	**finir**	**comprendre**

Passé Composé with **Avoir**

manger
travailler
acheter
casser
étudier
parler
pouvoir
devoir
vouloir
réussir
finir
comprendre

Passé Composé with **Être**

aller
tomber
partir
entrer
rester
retourner

Stressed Pronouns (Chapitre 13)

1. The following are some quotes that you could imagine hearing over the course of Jean and Aurélie's adventures. Draw lines to match the quotes on the left with the situation described on the right.

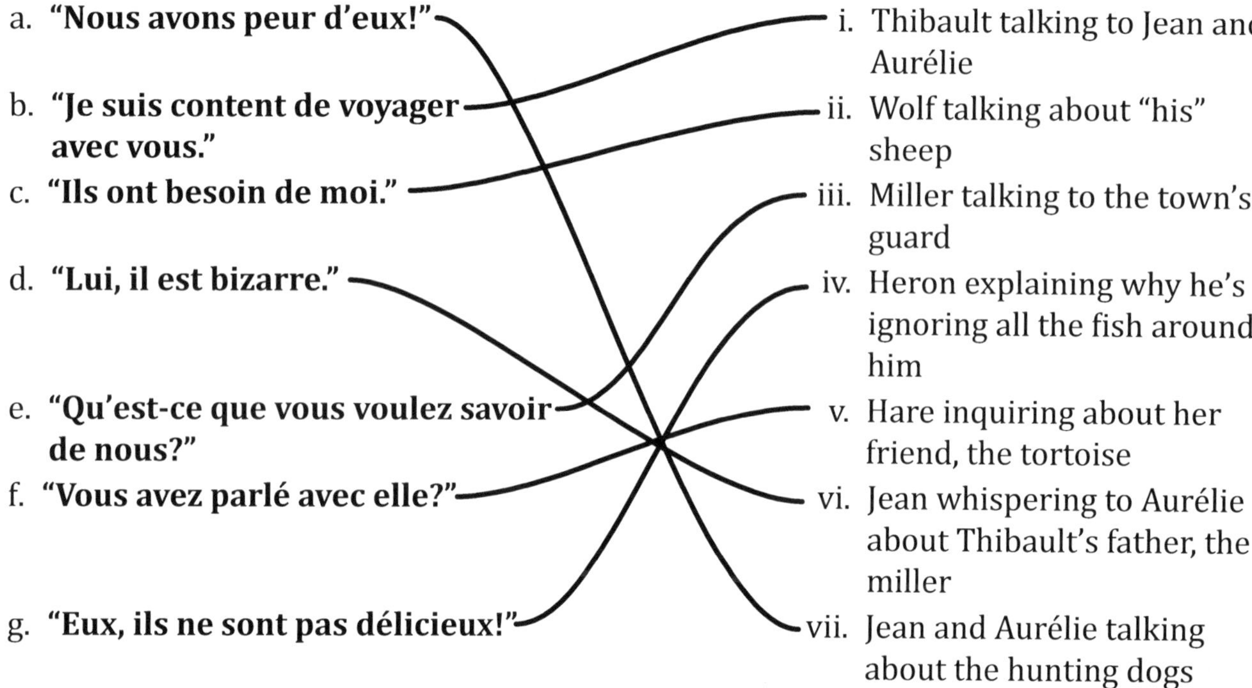

a. **"Nous avons peur d'eux!"**

b. **"Je suis content de voyager avec vous."**

c. **"Ils ont besoin de moi."**

d. **"Lui, il est bizarre."**

e. **"Qu'est-ce que vous voulez savoir de nous?"**

f. **"Vous avez parlé avec elle?"**

g. **"Eux, ils ne sont pas délicieux!"**

i. Thibault talking to Jean and Aurélie

ii. Wolf talking about "his" sheep

iii. Miller talking to the town's guard

iv. Heron explaining why he's ignoring all the fish around him

v. Hare inquiring about her friend, the tortoise

vi. Jean whispering to Aurélie about Thibault's father, the miller

vii. Jean and Aurélie talking about the hunting dogs

2. Now, translate the French sentences into English. There may be multiple ways to translate those sentences using stressed pronouns for emphasis.

   a. **"Nous avons peur d'eux!"** "We are afraid of them!"

   b. **"Je suis content de voyager avec vous."** "I am happy to travel with you."

   c. **"Ils ont besoin de moi."** "They need me."

   d. **"Lui, il est bizarre."** "Him, he's bizarre." *or* "*He's* bizarre" (with emphasis on the "he").

   e. **"Qu'est-ce que vous voulez savoir de nous?"** "What do you want to know about us?"

f. **"Vous avez parlé avec elle?"** "You spoke with her?"

g. **"Eux, ils ne sont pas délicieux!"** "Them, they're not delicious!" *or* "*They* are not delicious" (with emphasis on the "they").

Pronominal Verbs (Chapitre 14)

1. Look at the following English sentences. Circle the one which you could say using a *pronominal* verb in French (given the vocabulary you've learned in this book).

   a. The children left the school.

   b. I arrived late.

   c. She should take a break.

   (d.) We talked to each other this morning.

2. Again, which of the English sentences below could you say using a *pronominal* verb in French?

   (a.) They washed themselves in the river.

   b. I know your brother.

   c. They don't understand French.

   d. She's right. I run fast!

3. In each of the following conjugations, insert the correct reflexive pronoun.

   a. Je me couche. I go to bed.

   b. Tu te couches. You go to bed.

   c. Il se couche. He goes to bed.

   d. Elle se couche. She goes to bed.

   e. Nous nous couchons. We go to bed.

   f. Vous vous couchez. You go to bed.

   g. Ils se couchent. They go to bed.

   h. Elles se couchent. They go to bed.

Traduction

Translate the following English sentences into French, or vice versa.

1. **Il y a une forêt près de chez moi où j'aime me promener.**

   Translation: There is a forest near my house where I like to go for walks (or "for a walk").

2. Thibault, Jean, and Aurélie get up very late.

   Translation: **Thibault, Jean, et Aurélie se lèvent très tard.**

3. I like to brush my teeth.

   Translation: **J'aime me brosser les dents.**

4. His house is located near a big road.

   Translation: **Sa maison se trouve près d'une grande route.**

Past and Future Tenses + *ne . . . pas . . .* with Pronominal Verbs (Chapitre 15)

1. In French, the past tense (**passé composé**) is formed with a helping verb and a past participle. What is the helping verb with the past tense for *all* pronominal verbs?

   a. **avoir**

   b. **venir**

   c. **aller**

   (d.) **être**

2. The following sentences got jumbled around. Put the words of the French sentences in the correct order, and then translate each sentence into English.

   a. **la à enfants sont amusés se campagne les.**

   Correct Order: **Les enfants se sont amusés à la campagne.** *or* **À la campagne, les enfants se sont amusés.**

   Translation: **The children had fun in the countryside.** *or* **In the countryside, the children had fun.**

b. **est souvenu il s' moi de.**

Correct Order: **Il s'est souvenu de moi.**

Translation: **He remembered me.**

c. **pour à voyage 7 heures demain je me lever dois demain mon.**

Correct Order: **Je dois me lever à 7 heures pour mon voyage demain.** *or* **Demain, pour mon voyage, je dois me lever à 7 heures.**

Translation: **I have to get up at 7 o'clock for my trip tomorrow.** *or* **Tomorrow, for my trip, I have to get up at 7 o'clock.**

CHAPITRE 17 DIX-SEPT

Félicitations! (Congratulations!) You've made it! Here we are at the last chapter, **le dernier chapitre**, to take some time to review all that you've learned. This end-of-book review **chapitre** is organized according to the three units, or **parties**, of this book:

- **Partie** 1: Irregular Verbs, Negatives, and Question Formation
- **Partie** 2: Question Formation Part 2, Boot Verbs, and Future-Tense Verbs
- **Partie** 3: Past-Tense Verbs, Stressed Pronouns, and Pronominal Verbs

Plus, we'll have a final vocabulary review at the end just to make sure all of those new words are properly tucked away in the French-speaking corner of your brain.

Partie 1: Irregular Verbs, Negatives, and Question Formation

1. **Confused Conjugations:** Below are the conjugation charts for **être** and **avoir**, two of our irregular verbs. Some of the French forms have accidentally been switched from one chart to the other—and not necessarily to the same spot. Your job is to find the mix-ups, cross them out, and write the correct forms in the boxes.

Être (to be)

Person	Singular	Plural
1st Person	~~**je suis**~~ tu es (I am)	**nous sommes** ______ (we are)
2nd Person	**tu as** ______ (you are)	~~**vous êtes**~~ ils/elles sont (you are)
3rd Person	**il/elle est** ______ (he/she/it is)	**ils/elles ont** ______ (they are)

Avoir (to have)[1]

Person	Singular	Plural
1st Person	**j'ai** ____________ (I have)	**nous avons** ____________ (we have)
2nd Person	**tu as** ____________ (you have)	**vous avez** ____________ (you are)
3rd Person	~~**il/elle est**~~ il/elle a (he/she/it has)	~~**ils/elles sont**~~ ils/elles ont (they have)

2. Switch the following sentences around by making the positive sentences negative and the negative sentences positive. Then, translate what you've written into English.

   a. **Je n'ai pas de serpent.** I do not have a snake.

   Positive/Negative: J'ai un serpent.

   Translation: I have a snake.

   b. **Mon chat aime mon serpent.** My cat likes my snake.

   Positive/Negative: Mon chat n'aime pas mon serpent.

   Translation: My cat doesn't like my snake.

   c. **Le chat n'a pas peur de lui.** The cat is not afraid of him.

   Positive/Negative: Le chat a peur de lui.

   Translation: The cat is afraid of him.

---

1. You learned the conjugation of **avoir** in **chapitre** 8 of *FFCA*.

d. **Mon serpent ne veut pas manger mon chat.** My snake does not want to eat my cat.

Positive/Negative: Mon serpent veut manger mon chat.

Translation: My snake wants to eat my cat.

e. **Les animaux sont toujours très sympathiques.** Animals are always very nice.

Positive/Negative: Les animaux ne sont pas toujours très sympathiques.

Translation: Animals are not always very nice.

f. **Vraiment? Vous êtes d'accord?** Really? Do you agree?

Positive/Negative: Vraiment? Vous n'êtes pas d'accord?

Translation: Really? You don't agree?

3. The following questions are not entirely complete. Help finish them off by adding any words—or parts of words—that might be missing. There will only be one missing item per sentence. Then, translate each corrected sentence into English. An example has been provided to start you off.

Exemple: Pourquoi est- ce que vous voulez rester à la maison?

Translation: Why do you want to stay at home?

a. **Pourquoi est-ce** que **nous devons acheter douze sacs de pommes de terre?**

Translation: Why do we have to buy twelve bags of potatoes?

b. Quand est-ce que nous allons manger douze sacs de pommes de terre?
(When)

Translation: When are we going to eat twelve bags of potatoes?

c. **Comment est-ce que** nous **pouvons finir douze sacs?**

Translation: How can we finish twelve bags?

d. **Est-**ce **que tu connais une bonne recette pour les pommes de terre? (recette** = recipe)

Translation: Do you know a good recipe for potatoes?

e. Est **-ce que tes amis peuvent manger avec nous?**

Translation: Can your friends eat with us?

Partie 2: Question Formation Part 2, Boot Verbs, and Future-Tense Verbs

1. Circle the correct answer. What is the difference between these two questions: "Qui veut une cerise?" and "Qui est-ce qui veut une cerise?" **Who wants a cherry?**
   a. The first question is asking, "Who wants a cherry?" while the second is asking, "Who is who, and who wants a cherry?"
   (b.) The first question is essentially asking the same thing as the second question.
   c. The first question is asking, "Who wants a cherry?" while the second question asks, "Who would like a cherry?"
   d. The first question is asking, "Who wants a cherry?" and the second question asks, "Who is a cherry?"

2. Circle the correct answer. Which question will you *never* see in French?
   a. **Quand est-ce que tu veux manger?** When do you want to eat?
   b. **Qu'est-ce que tu veux manger?** What do you want to eat?
   c. **Où est-ce que tu veux manger?** Where do you want to eat?
   (d.) **Quoi est-ce que tu veux manger?**
3. Translate the following questions into French:
   a. "When can you (**tu**) come to my house?"

      Translation: **"Quand est-ce que tu peux venir à ma maison?"** *or* **"Quand est-ce que tu peux venir chez moi?"** (Note: The second option sounds more natural.)
   b. "What can we do at your house?"

      Translation: **"Qu'est-ce que nous pouvons faire à ta maison?"** *or* **"Qu'est-ce que nous pouvons faire chez toi?"**
   c. "What do you want to do?"

      Translation: **"Qu'est-ce que tu veux faire?"**
   d. "Can we play with the fish?"

      Translation: **"Est-ce que nous pouvons jouer avec le poisson/les poissons?"**
   e. "Do we have to play with fish?"

      Translation: **"Est-ce que nous devons jouer avec des poissons?"**
   f. "Who *doesn't* like playing with fish?"

      Translation: **"Qui n'aime pas jouer avec des poissons?"**
   g. "Are you crazy?"

      Translation: **"Est-ce que tu es fou?"**

4. On the left-hand side of the following chart there are French sentences followed by English translations. Using the left side of the chart as a guide, see if you can translate into French the English sentences on the right side of the chart.

Je ne vais pas manger mes légumes.
I'm not going to eat my vegetables.

a. I'm not going to look at my vegetables.

Translation: **Je ne vais pas regarder mes légumes.**

Nous allons chercher des fruits dans la forêt.
We're going to look for fruit in the woods.

b. We're going to find fruit in the forest.

Translation: **Nous allons trouver des fruits dans la forêt.**

Il ne va pas courir très loin.
He will not run very far.

c. He will not swim very far.

Translation: **Il ne va pas nager très loin.**

Vous allez avoir faim.
You will be hungry.

d. You won't be hungry.

Translation: **Vous n'allez pas avoir faim.**

Elles vont comprendre le musée.
They will understand the museum.

e. They won't understand the museum.

Translation: **Ils ne vont pas comprendre le musée.**

Je ne vais pas avoir peur de toi.
I will not be afraid of you.

f. You will be afraid of my cat.

Translation: **Tu vas avoir peur de mon chat.**

Partie 3: Past-Tense Verbs and Stressed Pronouns

1. Fill in the blanks. In French, the past tense is called the passé composé. It is made up of two parts. Do you remember the names of those parts? Identify them in the boxes below:

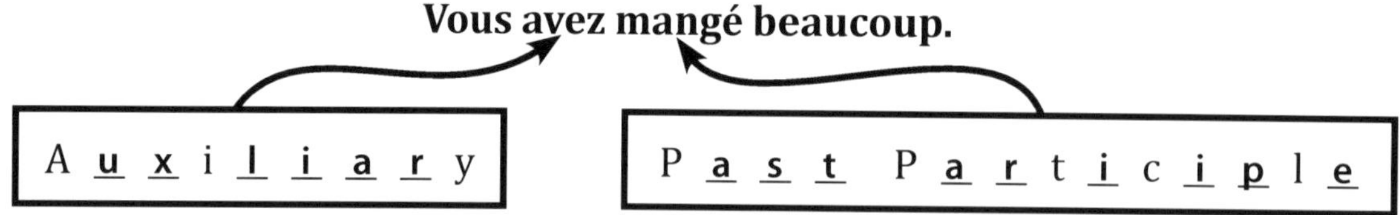

2. Draw lines between the following two columns to match the infinitives with their past-tense forms. We've done the first one for you. Then, once you've checked your answers, cover up the list and see if you can memorize them in two or three tries.

Infinitive	Past-Tense Form (or Past Participle)
chanter to sing	**dit** said
finir to finish	**pu** could
rencontrer to meet	**eu** had
devoir to have to, should	**allé** went
manger to eat	**fini** finished
pouvoir to be able to/can	**chanté** sang
aller to go	**été** was
être to be	**pensé** thought
faire to do/to make	**dû** had to/needed to
dire to say	**fait** did/made
penser to think	**rencontré** met
avoir to have	**mangé** ate

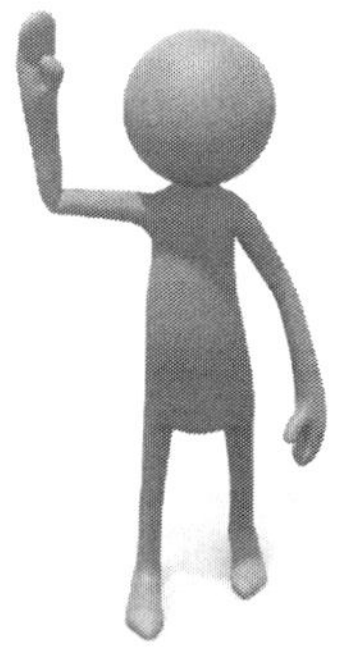

3. We've given you a choice of two options for how to translate the first few words of each of the following sentences. Circle the correct option, and then translate the rest of the sentence into French. Be sure to write the entire French sentence on the blank provided. Use the example as a guide:

Exemple: Our dog fell off the tree. (Notre chien est tombé / Notre chien a tombé)

Translation: **Notre chien est tombé de l'arbre.**

a. My mom left at eight o'clock with my brother.
(**Ma mère a parti** / **Ma mère est partie**)

Translation: **Ma mère est partie à huit heures avec mon frère.**

b. She went to the zoo with him. (**Elle est allée** / **Elle a allé**)

Translation: **Elle est allée au zoo avec lui.**

c. They looked at the snakes. (**Ils sont regardés** / **Ils ont regardé**)

Translation: **Ils ont regardé les serpents.**

d. My mom didn't like the snakes; she is afraid of them.
(**Ma mère n'est pas aimée** / **Ma mère n'a pas aimé**)

Translation: **Ma mère n'a pas aimé les serpents; elle a peur d'eux.**

e. Then they met a nice cow and, with her, a funny mouse.
(**Ensuite, ils sont rencontrés** / **Ensuite, ils ont rencontré**)

Translation: **Ensuite, ils ont rencontré une vache sympa et, avec elle, une souris amusante.**

f. But my mom and my brother thought that they were a little bizarre.
(**Mais ma mère et mon frère ont pensé** / **Mais ma mère et mon frère sont pensés**)

Translation: **Mais ma mère et mon frère ont pensé qu'elles ont été un peu bizarres.**

g. They spoke French! (**Elles sont parlés** / **Elles ont parlé**)

Translation: Elles ont parlé français!

4. Consider the pronominal verb **se souvenir** ("to remember"). How should we translate the reflexive pronouns (**me**, **te**, **se**, **nous**, **vous**, etc.) that are associated with this verb? For example, how would one translate the **me** in **je me souviens** or the **te** in **tu te souviens**? Circle the correct answer.

   a. The reflexive pronoun means "myself" or "yourself," as in: "I remember myself" or "You remember yourself."

   b. The reflexive pronoun has no single-word translation in this case—it is simply a part of the verb, and does not mean anything "extra." The translation would be "I remember" or "You remember."

   c. The reflexive pronoun means "each other" in this case, giving us, "I remember each other" or "You remember each other."

   d. The reflexive pronoun means the sentence is automatically in the past tense: "I remembered" or "You remembered."

A-Tense-Tion!

1. In the following table there are three columns. On the left is the past tense, in the middle is the present tense, and on the right is the future tense. For each row, use the sentence already there as a guide and then change the sentence into the other two tenses where the blanks remain. We've done the first line for you as an example.

Le Passé Composé	Le Présent	Le Futur
Elles se sont inquiétées.	**Elles s'inquiètent.**	**Elles vont s'inquiéter.**
Nous nous sommes brossés les dents.	Nous nous brossons les dents.	Nous allons nous brosser les dents.
Il s'est amusé.	**Il s'amuse.**	Il va s'amuser.

Le Passé Composé	Le Présent	Le Futur
Tu t'es occupé de moi.	Tu t'occupes de moi.	Tu vas t'occuper de moi.
Nous nous sommes habillés.	Nous nous habillons.	Nous allons nous habiller.
Elles se sont levées.	Elles se lèvent.	Elles vont se lever.

2. Now, translate the present-tense forms of the sentences from the table.

a. We are brushing our teeth.

b. He is having fun.

c. You are taking care of me.

d. We are getting dressed.

e. They are getting up.

Vocabulary Review

Try your hand at this final test of the vocabulary you've learned in this book. You should be able to score at least 75 percent on this test (though we hope it will be as close to 100 percent as possible!). If you don't score at least 75 percent, keep reviewing your vocabulary, and give it another try in a few days. The numbers after each word tell you from which chapter the word comes.

	French	English
☐	1. **avoir envie de, j'ai envie de (1)**	to feel like/to want, I feel like/I want
☐	2. **ensemble (1)**	together
☐	3. **un manteau (2)**	a coat
☐	4. **un chapeau (2)**	a hat
☐	5. **une chemise (2)**	a shirt
☐	6. **avoir l'air (de), j'ai l'air (de) (3)**	to seem (like), I seem (like)
☐	7. **ce (3)**	this, that
☐	8. **comme (3)**	like
☐	9. **être d'accord, je suis d'accord (4)**	to agree, I agree
☐	10. **le marché (4)**	the market

	French	English
☐	11. **un légume (4)**	a vegetable
☐	12. **faire, je fais (6)**	to do/to make, I do/I make
☐	13. **cacher, je cache (6)**	to hide (something), I hide (something)
☐	14. **devoir, je dois (7)**	to have to, should; I have to, I should
☐	15. **pouvoir, je peux (7)**	to be able to, I can
☐	16. **vouloir, je veux (7)**	to want, I want
☐	17. **une pomme de terre (7)**	a potato
☐	18. **venir, je viens (8)**	to come, I come
☐	19. **avoir raison/tort, j'ai raison/tort (8)**	to be right/wrong, I am right/wrong
☐	20. **dormir, je dors (8)**	to sleep, I sleep

	French	English
☐	21. **savoir, je sais (9)**	to know, I know
☐	22. **le pommier (9)**	the apple tree
☐	23. **prendre, je prends (9)**	to take, I take
☐	24. **demain (11)**	tomorrow
☐	25. **hier (11)**	yesterday
☐	26. **la semaine (11)**	the week
☐	27. **dire, je dis (12)**	to say, I say
☐	28. **un musée (12)**	a museum
☐	29. **ensuite (12)**	then, next
☐	30. **sans (13)**	without
☐	31. **un magasin (13)**	a store
☐	32. **s'habiller, je m'habille (14)**	to get dressed, I get dressed
☐	33. **se laver, je me lave (14)**	to wash (oneself), I wash myself
☐	34. **se trouver, je me trouve (14)**	to be located, I am located

	French	English
☐	35. **il y a (14)**	there is/there are
☐	36. **s'inquiéter (de), je m'inquiète (de) (15)**	to worry about, I worry about
☐	37. **s'occuper de, je m'occupe de (15)**	to take care of, I take care of
☐	38. **se souvenir (de), je me souviens (de) (15)**	to remember (**de** + something), I remember (**de** + something)
☐	39. **la campagne (15)**	the countryside
☐	40. **mieux (15)**	better

Chapitre 1

Français	Anglais
être, je suis	to be, I am
voyager, je voyage	to travel, I travel
visiter, je visite	to visit, I visit
avoir envie de, j'ai envie de	to feel like/to want, I feel like/I want
un endroit	a place
une idée	an idea
ensemble	together
intelligent/bête	smart/dumb
content/triste	happy/sad
difficile/simple	difficult/simple

Conversation Journal

C'est dommage.	That's a shame. *or* That's too bad.
où?	where?
un peu	a little (For example: I know a *little* German.)
si	so (as in "*so* nice" or "*so* sad")

Chapitre 2

Français	Anglais
aller, je vais	to go, I go
un manteau	a coat
un chapeau	a hat
une chemise	a shirt
un pantalon	pants
une chaussure/chaussette	a shoe, a sock
un mouton	a sheep
un berger	a shepherd
une foire	a fair
un loup	a wolf
porter, je porte	to wear, I wear (Note: You've already learned that the verb **porter** means "to carry." It can also mean "to wear" as in "to wear clothing.")

Conversation Journal

Vas-y!/Allez-y!	Go ahead!/Go on!/Keep going! (a kind of encouragement)
aujourd'hui	today
très bien	very good
ça	that/it (**C'est ça!** = That's it!)

Chapitre 3

Français	Anglais
avoir l'air (de), j'ai l'air (de)	to seem (like), I seem (like)
commencer, je commence	to begin/to start, I begin/I start
des vêtements	clothes
un sac	a bag
une patte	a paw, hoof, foot
une queue	a tail
une manière	a way, a manner
le pain	bread
ce	this, that
comme	like (ex., "He looks *like* you.")

Conversation Journal

puisque	since (ex., "We're tired *since* we didn't sleep last night.")
pas du tout	not at all

Chapitre 4

Français	Anglais
acheter, j'achète	to buy, I buy
entrer, j'entre	to enter, I enter
être d'accord, je suis d'accord	to agree, I agree
terminer, je termine	to terminate/finish, I terminate/finish
le marché	the market
un fruit	a fruit
un légume	a vegetable
une chose	a thing
fatigué	tired
encore	again, more

Conversation Journal

Quand?	When?
Entrez!	Come in!, Enter!
Assez!	Enough!

Chapitre 6

Français	Anglais
faire, je fais	to do/to make, I do/I make
arriver, j'arrive	to arrive, I arrive
cacher, je cache	to hide (something), I hide (something)
casser, je casse	to break, I break
tirer, je tire	to pull, I pull
dégoûtant	disgusting
l'œuf	the egg
l'omelette	the omelet
le rat	the rat
la dame	the lady

Conversation Journal

là	there (as in a place right around where you are speaking—"What are you doing *there*? That's my seat!" *not* "over there" [**là-bas**], which is farther away)
s'il vous plaît	please (formal or group)

Chapitre 7

Français	Anglais
devoir, je dois	to have to, should; I have to, I should
pouvoir, je peux	to be able to, I can
vouloir, je veux	to want, I want
cher	expensive
une pomme	an apple
une fraise	a strawberry
une pêche	a peach
une pomme de terre	a potato
une tomate	a tomato

Conversation Journal

je suis sûr	I'm sure
Pas de problème.	No problem.

Chapitre 8

Français	Anglais
attendre, j'attends	to wait, I wait
courir, je cours	to run, I run
dormir, je dors	to sleep, I sleep
avoir raison/tort, j'ai raison/tort	to be right/wrong, I am right/wrong
venir, je viens	to come, I come
une course	a race
une cerise	a cherry
une poire	a pear
fou	crazy
vite/lent	fast/slow

Conversation Journal

bon appétit	enjoy your meal (A common phrase to say at the beginning of a meal.)
pas grand-chose	nothing much
N'est-ce pas?	Right? as in "You're coming, *right*?" or "They won, *right*?"
déjà	already

Chapitre 9

Français	Anglais
comprendre, je comprends	to understand, I understand
prendre, je prends	to take, I take
voir, je vois	to see, I see
partir, je pars	to leave, I leave (location)
savoir, je sais	to know, I know (facts or abilities)
un raisin	a grape
une région	a region
souvent	often
le pommier	the apple tree
le cerisier	the cherry tree
la vigne	the vine

Conversation Journal

d'accord	OK, as in "OK, I agree," *not* as in "Are you OK?"
chez moi	at my house, my home, or more generally, "Where I am from."
non plus	neither/either, as in "Me neither" or "They don't understand either."

Chapitre II

Français	Anglais
connaître, je connais	to know, I know (personally)
gagner, je gagne	to win, I win
demain	tomorrow
avant	before
le soir	the evening
le matin	the morning
hier	yesterday
l'après-midi	the afternoon
la semaine	the week
tard	late

Conversation Journal

faire attention	to pay attention (ex. **Je fais attention** = I pay attention)
mademoiselle	miss (as in "Excuse me, Miss.")
cette	this, that (for feminine nouns; **ce**, from **chapitre** 3, is used for masculine nouns)
les jours de la semaine	the days of the week (Note that to say in French, "Today is Thursday"—or Friday, or Monday, etc.—we often say, "**Aujourd'hui, nous sommes jeudi**," which means "Today we are Thursday.")
Lundi, Mardi, Mercredi, Jeudi, Vendredi, Samedi, Dimanche	Monday, Tuesday, Wednesday, Thursday, Friday, Saturday, Sunday

Chapitre 12

Français	Anglais
rencontrer, je rencontre	to meet, I meet
dire, je dis	to say, I say
retourner, je retourne	to return, I return
un musée	a museum
un restaurant	a restaurant
ensuite	then, next
finalement	finally
seulement	only
jamais	never
après	after

Conversation Journal

Incroyable!	Unbelievable!
Chouette!	Awesome!
Laisse tomber!	Forget it! (The literal translation is "Let it fall!")

Chapitre 13

Français	Anglais
fermer, je ferme	to close, I close
faire une pause, je fais une pause	to take a break, I take a break
un voyage	a trip, a voyage
un magasin	a store
la route	the road
au milieu de	in the middle of
sans	without
sous	under
normal	normal
la fin	the end

Conversation Journal

Bonne soirée.	Have a good evening/night.
Mince!	Darn!
Félicitations!	Congratulations!
entre nous	between us *or* just between us (Note the preposition **entre**, which means "between.")

Chapitre 14

Français	Anglais
s'habiller, je m'habille	to get dressed, I get dressed
se brosser (les dents), je me brosse (les dents)	to brush (your teeth), I brush (my teeth)
se coucher, je me couche	to go to bed, I go to bed
se laver, je me lave	to wash (oneself), I wash myself
se lever, je me lève	to get up, I get up
se promener, je me promène	to go for a walk, I go for a walk
se trouver, je me trouve	to be located, I am located
même	same
quelque chose	something/anything
il y a	there is/there are
une dent	a tooth

Conversation Journal

parfait	perfect
ça alors!	an expression of surprise, and sometimes surprised disapproval—used like the English expressions "No way!" or "Get out of here!" or "Well, really!"

Chapitre 15

Français	Anglais
s'amuser, je m'amuse	to have fun, I have fun
se dépêcher, je me dépêche	to hurry, I hurry
s'endormir, je m'endors	to fall asleep, I fall asleep
s'inquiéter (de), je m'inquiète (de)	to worry (about), I worry (about)
s'occuper de, je m'occupe de	to take care of, I take care of
se sentir, je me sens	to feel, I feel
se souvenir (de), je me souviens (de)	to remember (**de** + something), I remember (**de** + something)
fort	strong (can also mean "good" or "capable" as a more familiar, colloquial expression—see dialogue)
la campagne	the countryside
mieux	better

Conversation Journal

purée!	An exclamation of surprise, such as "Oh man!" or "Holy smokes!"

Alphabetical Vocabulaire

Note: This glossary contains, in alphabetical order, all of the vocabulary words from *French for Children Primers A* and *B*. In this glossary, all nouns are designated as masculine *(m.)* or feminine *(f.)*. The abbreviation *CJ* applies to words that appear in the Conversation Journal section of the indicated chapter. Articles (**le**, **la**, etc.) have been omitted.

Français (French)	**Anglais** (English)	**Chapitre** (Chapter)	
		FFCA	***FFCB***
à	to, at	1	
à côté de	next to	6	
acheter, j'achète	to buy, I buy		4
adieu	farewell	15 (CJ)	
aimer, j'aime	to like/love, I like/love	2	
aller, je vais	to go, I go		2
Allons-y!	Let's go!	2 (CJ)	
alors	so (used very often in conversation, such as "*So*, you want to go fishing?")	1 (CJ)	
ami (m.)	friend	9	
amusant	funny	12	
s'amuser, je m'amuse[1]	to have fun, I have fun		15
âne (m.)	donkey	15	
animal (m.)	animal	9	
après	after		12
après-midi (m.)	afternoon		11
arbre (m.)	tree	4	
arriver, j'arrive	to arrive, I arrive		6
Assez!	Enough!		4 (CJ)
attendre, j'attends	to wait, I wait		8
Attention!	Careful!	11 (CJ)	
au milieu de	in the middle of		13
au revoir	good-bye	4 (CJ)	
aujourd'hui	today		2 (CJ)
aussi	too, also	8 (CJ)	
avant	before		11

1. It is common practice in French dictionaries to keep the se or s' in front of the verb, but to alphabetize the verb itself by the main root.

Français (French)	**Anglais** (English)	**Chapitre** (Chapter) *FFCA*	*FFCB*
avec	with	1	
avoir, j'ai	to have, I have	8	
avoir besoin de, j'ai besoin de	to need, I need	12	
avoir envie de, j'ai envie de	to feel like/to want, I feel like/I want		1
avoir faim, j'ai faim	to be hungry, I am hungry	9	
avoir l'air (de), j'ai l'air (de)	to seem (like), I seem (like)		3
avoir peur de, j'ai peur de	to be afraid of, I'm afraid of	11	
avoir raison/tort, j'ai raison/tort	to be right/wrong, I am right/wrong		8
beau	handsome	14	
beaucoup	a lot, many, very much	2	
belle	beautiful	14	
ben	This word is used in the same way we use the English word "well" when we don't know exactly what to say in a conversation. For example: "*Well*, I guess you can wear a bathing suit to the movies if you really want . . ." or "*Well*, I'm not sure what I'd do if my refrigerator exploded!"	2 (CJ)	
berger (m.)	shepherd		2
bien sûr	of course	2 (CJ)	
bientôt	soon	6 (CJ)	
bienvenue	welcome (as in "You are welcome here.")	7 (CJ)	
bizarre	bizarre	13	
blanc	white	12	
bleu	blue	12	
bon	good	14	
bon appétit	enjoy your meal (Used between friends/family much more often in French than in English!)		8 (CJ)
bonne chance	good luck	12 (CJ)	
Bonne soirée.	Have a good evening/night.		13 (CJ)
bonsoir	good evening	4 (CJ)	
bouche (f.)	mouth	14	
bras (m.)	arm	15	

Français (French)	**Anglais** (English)	**Chapitre** (Chapter) *FFCA*	*FFCB*
se brosser (les dents), je me brosse (les dents)	to brush (your teeth), I brush (my teeth)		14
c'est	that is, that's, this is	14 (CJ)	
C'est dommage.	That's a shame. *or* That's too bad.		1 (CJ)
ça	that/it (**C'est ça!** = That's it!)		2 (CJ)
ça alors!	an expression of surprise, and sometimes surprised disapproval—used like the English expressions "No way!" or "Get out of here!" or "Well, really!"		14 (CJ)
ça va	This phrase can be a question, such as "How are you?" "How are things going?" "How is it going?" or "Is everything OK?" It can also be an answer, such as "I'm doing fine" or "Things are going well." It all depends on how you say it—with a questioning tone of voice or with an answering tone of voice.	1 (CJ)	
cacher, je cache	to hide (something), I hide (something)		6
cadeau (m.)	present, gift	9	
campagne (f.)	countryside		15
carte (f.)	map	1	
casser, je casse	to break, I break		6
ce	this, that		3
cerise (f.)	cherry		8
cerisier (m.)	cherry tree		9
cette	this, that (for feminine nouns; **ce**, from **chapitre** 3, is used for masculine nouns)		11 (CJ)
champ (m.)	field	7	
chanter, je chante	to sing, I sing	4	
chapeau (m.)	hat		2
chat (m.)	cat	3	
chaussure/chaussette (f.)	shoe, sock		2
chemise (f.)	shirt		2
cher	expensive		7
chercher, je cherche	to look (for), I look (for)	3	
cheval (m.)	horse	9	
cheveux (m.)	hair	14	

Français (French)	**Anglais** (English)	**Chapitre** (Chapter)	
		FFCA	*FFCB*
chez moi	at my house, my home, or more generally, "Where I am from."		9 (CJ)
chien (m.)	dog	3	
chose (f.)	thing		4
Chouette!	Awesome!		12 (CJ)
Chut!	Shhhh!, Be quiet!	1 (CJ)	
Ciao!	See you!/See you later! (pronounced CHOW)	7 (CJ)	
cinq	five	8	
cochon (m.)	pig	6	
combien	how many *or* how much (as in a question)	9 (CJ)	
comme	like (ex., "He looks *like* you.")		3
commencer, je commence	to begin/to start, I begin/I start		3
comment	This word can mean "how" as in the question, "How do you know?" but it can also mean, "Excuse me?"—a question one asks when one does not understand something.	3 (CJ)	
Comment t'appelles-tu?	What is your name?	4 (CJ)	
comprendre, je comprends	to understand, I understand		9
connaître, je connais	to know, I know (personally)		11
content/triste	happy/sad		1
se coucher, je me couche	to go to bed, I go to bed		14
courir, je cours	to run, I run		8
course (f.)	race		8
d'accord	OK, as in "OK, I agree," *not* as in "Are you OK?"		9 (CJ)
dame (f.)	lady		6
dans	in	4	
de	of, from	2	
de rien	you're welcome	9 (CJ)	
dégoûtant	disgusting		6
déjà	already		8 (CJ)
délicieux	delicious	12	
demain	tomorrow		11
dent	tooth		14

Français (French)	**Anglais** (English)	**Chapitre** (Chapter) *FFCA*	*FFCB*
se dépêcher, je me dépêche	to hurry, I hurry		15
derrière	behind	7	
désolé	sorry	3 (CJ)	
deux	two	8	
devant	in front of	6	
devoir (m.)	homework	2	
devoir, je dois	to have to, should; I have to, I should		7
difficile/simple	difficult/simple		1
dire, je dis	to say, I say		12
dix	ten	8	
dormir, je dors	to sleep, I sleep		8
dos (m.)	back	15	
douze	twelve	8	
eau (f.)	water	11	
école (f.)	school	2	
enchanté	nice to meet you	4 (CJ)	
encore	again, more		4
s'endormir, je m'endors	to fall asleep, I fall asleep		15
endroit (m.)	place		1
enfant (m.)	child	8	
ensemble	together		1
ensuite	then, next		12
entre nous	between us *or* just between us (Note preposition **entre**, which means "between.")		13 (CJ)
entrer, j'entre	to enter, I enter		4
Entrez!	Come in!, Enter!		4 (CJ)
épaule (f.)	shoulder	15	
espérer [que], j'espère [que]	to hope [that], I hope [that]	3	
et	and	1	
être d'accord, je suis d'accord	to agree, I agree		4
être, je suis	to be, I am		1
étudier, j'étudie	to study, I study	1	
excusez-moi	excuse me	11 (CJ)	

Français (French)	**Anglais** (English)	**Chapitre** (Chapter)	
		FFCA	*FFCB*
facile	easy	12	
faire attention	to pay attention (ex. **Je fais attention** = I pay attention)		11 (CJ)
faire une pause, je fais une pause	to take a break, I take a break		13
faire, je fais	to do/to make, I do/I make		6
famille (f.)	family	8	
fatigué	tired		4
Félicitations!	Congratulations!		13 (CJ)
femme (f.)	woman, wife	13	
ferme (f.)	farm	6	
fermer, je ferme	to close, I close		13
fille (f.)	girl, daughter	8, 13	
fils (m.)	son	13	
fin (f.)	end		13
finalement	finally		12
finir, je finis	to finish, I finish	3	
fleur (f.)	flower	7	
fleuve (m.)	river	11	
foire (f.)	fair		2
forêt (f.)	forest	2	
fort	strong (can also mean “good” or “capable” as a more familiar, colloquial expression)		15
fou	crazy		8
fraise (f.)	strawberry		7
français (m.)	French	1	
frère (m.)	brother	8	
fromage (m.)	cheese	6	
fruit (m.)	fruit		4
gagner, je gagne	to win, I win		11
garçon (m.)	boy	8	
Génial!	Great!		7 (CJ)
genou (m.)	knee	15	
gentil	nice/kind	12	
grand	big	14	
grange (f.)	barn	6	
s’habiller, je m’habille	to get dressed, I get dressed		14

Français (French)	**Anglais** (English)	**Chapitre** (Chapter)	
		FFCA	***FFCB***
habiter, j'habite	to live, I live	4	
heureux	happy	13	
hier	yesterday		11
homme (m.)	man	13	
huit	eight	8	
ici	here	4	
idée (f.)	idea		1
il y a	there is/there are		14
Incroyable!	Unbelievable!		12 (CJ)
s'inquiéter (de), je m'inquiète (de)	to worry (about), I worry (about)		15
intelligent/bête	smart/dumb		1
intéressant	interesting	12	
J'espère que oui.	I hope so.	6 (CJ)	
jamais	never		12
jambe (f.)	leg	15	
jaune	yellow	12	
je m'appelle	my name is	4 (CJ)	
Je pense que oui.	I think so.	6 (CJ)	
je suis sûr	I'm sure		7 (CJ)
jeu (m.)	game	9	
jeune	young	14	
jouer, je joue	to play, I play	6	
les jours de la semaine	days of the week (Note that to say in French, "Today is Thursday"—or Friday, or Monday, etc.—we often say, "**Aujourd'hui, nous sommes jeudi,**" which means "Today *we are* Thursday.")		11 (CJ)
là	there (as in a place right around where you are speaking—"What are you doing *there*? That's my seat!" *not* "over there" [**là-bas**], which is farther away)		6 (CJ)
La vache!	Holy cow!	8 (CJ)	
là-bas	over there	13 (CJ)	
se laver, je me lave	to wash (oneself), I wash myself		14
lac (m.)	lake	11	
Laisse tomber!	Forget it! (literal translation: "Let it fall!")		12 (CJ)
laisser, je laisse	to leave (something or someone), I leave (something or someone)	13	

Français (French)	**Anglais** (English)	**Chapitre** (Chapter) *FFCA*	*FFCB*
légume (m.)	vegetable		4
se lever, je me lève	to get up, I get up		14
loin (de)	far (from)	7	
loup (m.)	wolf		2
Lundi, Mardi, Mercredi, Jeudi, Vendredi, Samedi, Dimanche	Monday, Tuesday, Wednesday, Thursday, Friday, Saturday, Sunday		11 (CJ)
mademoiselle	miss (as in "Excuse me, miss.")		11 (CJ)
magasin (m.)	store		13
magnifique	magnificent, wonderful	12	
main/mains (f.)	hand/hands	15	
maintenant	now	12 (CJ)	
mais	but	9	
maison (f.)	house, home	2	
manger, je mange	to eat, I eat	3	
manière (f.)	way, manner		3
manteau (m.)	coat		2
marché (m.)	market		4
marcher, je marche	to walk, I walk	2	
matin (m.)	morning		11
mauvais	bad	14	
méchant	mean	12	
même	same		14
mer (f.)	sea	11	
merci	thank you	7 (CJ)	
mère (f.)	mother	8	
mieux	better		15
mignon	cute	13	
Mince!	Darn!		13 (CJ)
moche	ugly	13	
moi	me	12 (CJ)	
montagne (f.)	mountain	7	
mouton (m.)	sheep		2
musée (m.)	museum		12

Français (French)	**Anglais** (English)	**Chapitre** (Chapter) *FFCA*	*FFCB*
N'est-ce pas?	Right? as in "You're coming, *right*?" or "They won, *right*?"		8 (CJ)
nager, je nage	to swim, I swim	11	
neuf	nine	8	
nez (m.)	nose	14	
noir	black	12	
non	no	1 (CJ)	
non plus	neither/either, as in "Me neither" or "They don't understand either."		9 (CJ)
normal	normal		13
s'occuper de, je m'occupe de	to take care of, I take care of		15
œil/yeux (m.)	eye/eyes	14	
œuf (m.)	egg		6
oiseau (m.)	bird	7	
omelette (f.)	omelet		6
onze	eleven	8	
orange	orange	12	
oreille/oreilles (f.)	ear/ears	14	
ou	or	3	
où?	where?		1 (CJ)
oui	yes	1 (CJ)	
pain (m.)	bread		3
pantalon (m.)	pants		2
parce que	because	9 (CJ)	
paresseux	lazy	12	
parfait	perfect		14 (CJ)
parler, je parle	to speak, I speak	1	
partir, je pars	to leave, I leave (location)		9
Pas de problème.	no problem		7 (CJ)
pas du tout	not at all		3 (CJ)
pas grand-chose	nothing much		8 (CJ)
patte (f.)	paw, hoof, foot		3
pêche (f.)	peach		7
penser [que], je pense [que]	to think [that], I think [that]	4	

Français (French)	**Anglais** (English)	**Chapitre** (Chapter) *FFCA*	*FFCB*
père (m.)	father	8	
petit	small	14	
peut-être	perhaps, maybe	12 (CJ)	
pied (m.)	foot	15	
plage (f.)	beach	11	
poire (f.)	pear		8
poisson (m.)	fish	11	
pomme (f.)	apple		7
pomme de terre (f.)	potato		7
pommier (m.)	apple tree		9
porter, je porte	to carry, I carry *or* to wear, I wear	15	
pour	for	2	
pourquoi?	why?	15 (CJ)	
pouvoir, je peux	to be able to, I can		7
préférer, je préfère	to prefer, I prefer	4	
prendre, je prends	to take, I take		9
près (de)	near (to), close (to)	11	
problème (m.)	problem	9	
se promener, je me promène	to go for a walk, I go for a walk		14
puisque	since (ex., "We're tired *since* we didn't sleep last night.")		3 (CJ)
purée!	an exclamation of surprise such as "Oh man!" or "Holy smokes!"		15 (CJ)
Quand?	When?		4 (CJ)
quatre	four	8	
Quel âge as-tu?	How old are you?	14 (CJ)	
quelque chose	something/anything		14
queue (f.)	tail		3
qui?	who?	13 (CJ)	
quoi?	what?	13 (CJ)	
raisin (m.)	grape		9
rat (m.)	rat		6
regarder, je regarde	to look (at), I look (at)	1	
région (f.)	region		9
renard (m.)	fox	6	

Français (French)	**Anglais** (English)	**Chapitre** (Chapter) *FFCA*	*FFCB*
rencontrer, je rencontre	to meet, I meet		12
restaurant (m.)	restaurant		12
rester, je reste	to stay, I stay	3	
retourner, je retourne	to return, I return		12
réussir, je réussis	to succeed, I succeed	3	
rouge	red	12	
route (f.)	road		13
s'il te plaît	please (informal)	8 (CJ)	
s'il vous plaît	please (formal or group)		6 (CJ)
sac (m.)	bag		3
sans	without		13
savoir, je sais	to know, I know (facts or abilities)		9
semaine (f.)	week		11
se sentir, je me sens	to feel, I feel		15
sept	seven	8	
serpent (m.)	snake	6	
seulement	only		12
si	if, so (as in "*so* nice" *or* "*so* sad")	9	7
six	six	8	
sœur (f.)	sister	8	
soir (m.)	evening		11
souris (f.)	mouse	1	
sous	under		13
se souvenir (de), je me souviens (de)	to remember (**de** + something), I remember (**de** + something)		15
souvent	often		9
sur	on, on top of	7	
sympathique (sympa)	nice	12	
tard	late		11
terminer, je termine	to terminate/finish, I terminate/finish		4
tête (f.)	head	14	
tirer, je tire	to pull, I pull		6
tomate (f.)	tomato		7
tomber, je tombe	to fall, I fall	7	
toujours	always	9	
tout	everything, all	11	

Français (French)	Anglais (English)	Chapitre (Chapter) FFCA	FFCB
tout le monde	everyone, everybody	14 (CJ)	
travailler, je travaille	to work, I work	2	
très	very	13	
très bien	very good		2 (CJ)
trois	three	8	
trop	too (as in "too much," not as in "also")	15	
trouver, je trouve	to find, I find	4	
se trouver, je me trouve	to be located, I am located		14
un	one	8	
un peu	a little (For example, "I know a *little* German.")		1 (CJ)
vache (f.)	cow	1	
Vas-y!/Allez-y!	Go ahead!/Go on!/Keep going! (a kind of encouragement)		2 (CJ)
venir, je viens	to come, I come		8
vent (m.)	wind	7	
vers	toward	4	
vert	green	12	
vêtements (m.)	clothes		3
vieux	old	14	
vigne (f.)	vine		9
village (m.)	village	6	
ville (f.)	city	6	
violet	purple	12	
visiter, je visite	to visit, I visit		1
vite/lent	fast/slow		8
voilà	there it is, there you have it, there is, there we go	6 (CJ)	
voir, je vois	to see, I see		9
voiture (f.)	car	3	
voler, je vole	to fly, I fly	7	
vouloir, je veux	to want, I want		7
voyage (m.)	trip, voyage		13
voyager, je voyage	to travel, I travel		1
vraiment	really	13 (CJ)	
zoo (m.)	zoo	4	

Appendix A
Dialogue Translations

Chapitre 1

Dialogue [01_01/Tr. 1]

In case you're just joining us or can't quite recall what was happening in the dialogue sections in FFCA, *we have been following the story of Jean, a field mouse, and Aurélie, a dairy cow, who were mistakenly released into the wild after zookeepers mistook them for protected species. They have been trying to find their way back to the zoo and at this point in the story have joined up with a somewhat eccentric village miller and his son. The miller and his son are on their way to the local fair, which happens to be on the way to the city.*

Aurélie, Jean, the miller's son, and the miller—still carrying his donkey—set off for the fair. The miller manages to walk at a surprising pace, given his load, and soon he has gone some distance ahead of the others. Jean and Aurélie begin talking with the boy as the miles go by.

JEAN, *speaking to the miller's son.* **Alors! Comment t'appelles-tu?** (So! What's your name?)

THIBAULT. **Je m'appelle Thibault—et vous? Comment vous appelez-vous?** (My name is Thibault—and you? What are your names?)

JEAN. **Moi, je m'appelle Jean.** (Me, my name is Jean.)

AURÉLIE. **Et je suis Aurélie—enchantée!** (And I'm Aurélie—pleased to meet you!)

THIBAULT. **Enchanté! Je suis content de marcher avec vous.** (Pleased to meet you! I'm happy to walk with you.)

JEAN. **Nous sommes contents aussi.** (We're happy, too.) The road is a long one, and we're glad for the company. Plus, we weren't quite sure we could trust your dad's . . . errr . . . well . . . judgment. . . . *Jean points ahead to the miller, who is still huffing and puffing as he carries his donkey.*

THIBAULT. **Ah non, ça va, ça va. Il aime ses animaux, c'est tout. Et il aime beaucoup son âne!** (Oh, no, it's OK, it's OK. He loves animals, that's all. And he really loves his donkey!) He's just making sure it doesn't get too tired.

JEAN. Well, it's still nice to go along with you.

AURÉLIE. **Et vraiment . . . nous avons un peu peur de voyager . . . nous habitons dans le zoo!** (And really . . . we're a little scared of traveling . . . we live in the zoo!)

JEAN. Yes, you see, and we are not used to traveling like most folks. **Toi, tu voyages beaucoup?** (Do you travel a lot?)

THIBAULT. **Non. C'est dommage. J'ai envie de voyager. J'ai envie de visiter beaucoup d'endroits.** (No. It's too bad. I want to travel. I want to visit lots of places.)

AURÉLIE, *not believing that people actually want to travel on purpose.* **Vraiment? Où?** (*Really? Where?*)

THIBAULT. Oh, I don't know. **Beaucoup d'endroits sont intéressants . . . la plage, les montagnes . . . la ville, peut-être? Tout le monde dans mon village parle de la grande ville. "Oh, la ville, elle est magnifique!"** (Lots of places are interesting . . . the beach, the mountains . . . the city, maybe? Everyone in my village talks about the big city. "Oh, the city, it's great!") They say, "**La ville, elle est grande et belle!** (The city, it's big and beautiful!)" The farthest I've been, though, is just the next town over where the market is, so how should I know? **Mais vous, vous êtes de là-bas. Vous pensez que la ville est si belle?** (But you, you're from there. Do you think the city is so beautiful?)

JEAN. **Hmmm . . . tu as des bonnes questions.** (Hmmm . . . you have good questions.) You know, it's been so long since I was out walking around there. **Nous sommes toujours dans le zoo, alors c'est difficile pour nous d'avoir une idée.** (We're always in the zoo, so it's hard for us to have any idea.)

AURÉLIE. **J'ai une idée.** (I have an idea.)

THIBAULT AND JEAN. What is it?

AURÉLIE. **Nous visitons la ville ensemble!** (We visit the city together!)

THIBAULT. Hey, Jean, what do you think of that?

JEAN. **Oui! Je pense que c'est une bonne idée. Aurélie, tu es une vache intelligente!** (Yes! I think it's a good idea. Aurelie, you're an intelligent cow!) But I'm afraid it will be quite a challenge getting back . . . **si nous réussissons** (if we succeed), I'll be glad to see the city **avec toi, Thibault! Allons-y!** (with you, Thibault! Let's go!)

Chapitre 2

Dialogue [02_01/Tr. 8]

Suddenly, the miller stops dead in his tracks and cries out. The three companions soon catch up and see, approaching in the distance, the outline of a wolf walking toward them. As he nears, however, the four travelers realize that this is no ordinary predator.

THIBAULT. **Bonjour, Monsieur le Loup. Ça va?** (Hello, Mr. Wolf. How's it going?)

Monsieur le Loup. Ça va très bien, merci! Et vous, les amis? Vous allez où aujourd'hui? Vous allez aussi aux champs, peut-être? (Very well, thank you! And you, friends? Where are you going today? You're going to the fields, too, perhaps?)

Jean. **Aux champs? Non . . . nous allons à la foire . . .** (To the fields? No . . . we're going to the fair.)

Monsieur le Loup, *relieved.* **Aha! Ça c'est *très, très* bien.** (Aha! That's *very, very* good.) The fields are so boring, anyway.

Aurélie. **Mais, monsieur? Alors, pourquoi vous allez aux champs?** (But, sir? Then why are you going to the fields?)

Monsieur le Loup. Moi? Euh . . . je vais aux champs pour . . . euh . . . pour le business . . . oui, c'est ça. (Me? Um . . . I'm going to the fields for . . . um . . . for business . . . yes, that's it.)

Jean, *noticing the wolf's peculiar attire.* I see. **Mais j'ai une question. Pourquoi portez-vous un manteau?** (But I have a question. Why are you wearing a coat?)

Monsieur le Loup. Ah, mon manteau . . . alors . . . ça . . . (Oh, my coat . . . well . . . that . . .)

Thibault. **Oui, Monsieur le Loup . . . et vous portez aussi un chapeau? Les loups portent des chapeaux?** (Yes, Mr. Wolf . . . and you're also wearing a hat? Do wolves wear hats?)

Monsieur le Loup. Mon chapeau? Alors, c'est pour . . . euh . . . (My hat? Well, it's for . . . um . . .)

Thibault. And it looks like something's written on your hat, too—**"Je suis Guillaume, le berger des moutons." Monsieur? Vous êtes berger?** ("I'm William, the shepherd of the sheep." Sir? You're a shepherd?)

Monsieur le Loup. Oui . . . euh . . . oui! Et bien sûr, je m'appelle . . . Gérald—non—Guillaume! Je vais aux champs pour regarder mes moutons. (Yes . . . um . . . yes! And of course my name is . . . Gerald—no—William! I'm going to the fields to look at my sheep.)

Aurélie. **Oh, il est très intéressant, le loup. J'ai envie d'aller avec Guillaume!** (Oh, he's very interesting, this wolf. I'd like to go with William!)

Monsieur le Loup. Avec qui? Ah, non, non, non! C'est une mauvaise idée . . . (With who? Oh, no, no, no! That's a bad idea . . .) besides, **tu vas à la foire** (you're going to the fair); I don't want to make you late . . . **vas-y, vas-y** (go on, go on)!

Jean, *growing more and more suspicious.* **Alors, Guillaume. Vous aimez être berger?** (So, William. Do you like being a shepherd?)

Monsieur le Loup. Moi? Ah oui. (Me? Oh yes.) [*smiles*] **J'aime les moutons. Ils sont filets mignons—mmm ahem—** (I like the sheep. They're filets mignons—ahem—) [*coughs*] **excusez-moi—*très* mignons . . .** (excuse me—*very* cute . . .)

Chapitre 3

Dialogue [03_01/Tr. 14]

Jean, *who has had enough of the wolf's story.* **Monsieur le Loup, excusez-moi, mais nous ne sommes pas bêtes. Vous n'êtes pas berger.** (Mr. Wolf, excuse me, but we're not dumb. You're not a shepherd.)

Monsieur le Loup, *laughing nervously.* **Bien sûr, vous n'êtes pas bêtes, ou stupides . . .** (Of course, you aren't dumb, or stupid . . .) but you really don't think that I'm a shepherd? **Ha ha . . . alors, pourquoi pensez-vous que je ne suis pas berger?** (Ha ha . . . so, why do you think I'm not a shepherd?)

Le meunier. Well, your appearance, for one. **Vous n'avez pas l'air d'un berger.** (You don't seem like a shepherd.)

Monsieur le Loup. I don't seem like a shepherd? **Aha . . . ben, c'est normal . . . puisque je suis nouveau. . . .** (Aha . . . well, that's normal . . . because I'm new at it. . . .)

Thibault. Hmm . . . I'm not sure I believe that one, either. **En plus, vous ne marchez pas comme un berger. Ce n'est pas leur manière de marcher à quatre pattes.** (And furthermore, you aren't walking like a shepherd. It's not their style to walk on four paws.)

Monsieur le Loup. Vraiment . . . euh . . . (Really . . . um . . .)

Jean. **Vous ne portez pas des vêtements de berger. Votre manteau, c'est un grand sac! Où est votre pantalon? Où sont vos chaussures?** (You're not wearing shepherd's clothes. Your coat, it's a big bag! Where are your pants? Where are your shoes?)

Monsieur le Loup. Well, I mean, I have them, they're just back in my—

Aurélie, *realizing what's happening.* **Oh là là! Vous ne parlez pas comme un berger! Pas du tout!** (Oh my! You don't speak like a shepherd! Not at all!)

Monsieur le Loup. Je ne parle pas comme un berger? Comment? (I don't speak like a shepherd? Excuse me?) How do you know that?

Aurélie. **Puisque votre manière de parler n'est pas gentille.** (Because your way of talking isn't nice.)

Monsieur le Loup, *backing away slowly.* Well, friends, you'll have to excuse me—I really must be going. **Mes moutons sont délicieux**—ahem!—**un peu vieux, et ils ont besoin de moi pour trouver la grange . . .** (My sheep are delicious—ahem!—a little old, and they need me to find the barn . . .)

Jean. **Bien sûr.** (Of course.) Be off! But don't think that your costume is going to fool any sheep—let alone a real shepherd and his dogs. Besides, **les bergers n'ont pas de queue** (shepherds don't have tails)**!**

Monsieur le Loup, *shouts as he is running away.* We'll see! **J'espère que les moutons ne sont pas intelligents comme vous!** (I hope that the sheep aren't intelligent like you!)

Chapitre 4

Dialogue [04_01/Tr. 26]

At the end of the first leg of their long journey, the four travelers finally reach the town hosting the market. But even as they approach, the gatekeeper at the main entrance grows increasingly suspicious. He doesn't like the look of our four voyagers, and he has no shortage of questions for them upon their arrival. . . .

Le gardien (The Gatekeeper), *motions to the travelers to come off the road next to his watchtower; a huge, growling dog stands at his side.* Over here, **s'il vous plaît!** (please!)

Aurélie, *whispers to Jean.* **Oh là là, il a l'air méchant.** (Oh my, he seems mean.)

Jean, *whispering back.* **Je suis d'accord!** (I agree!)

Le gardien. Quoi!? Est-ce que tu parles de moi? (What!? Are you talking about me?)

Jean. **Non, monsieur.** (No, sir.)

Le gardien. J'espère que non. (I hope not.)

Jean. **Elle . . . elle . . . elle parle de votre chien. Elle pense qu'il est mignon.** (She . . . she . . . was talking about your dog. She thinks he's cute.)

Le gardien. Bruno!? Mignon!? Hmph . . . (Bruno!? Cute!? Hmph . . .), *forgetting his job for a moment,* **Je ne pense pas, mais peut-être. Il a des beaux yeux. Et ses pattes . . . elles sont mignonnes . . . Hum hum!** (I don't think so, but maybe. He has beautiful eyes. And his paws . . . they're cute . . . Ahem!) *remembering his duty,* **Où est-ce que vous allez?** (Where are you going?)

Le meunier. Ben, nous allons au marché, monsieur. (Well, we're going to the market, sir.)

Le gardien. Et pourquoi est-ce que vous allez à notre marché? (And why are you going to our market?)

Le meunier. Parce que nous avons envie d'acheter des choses ici. S'il vous plaît, Monsieur, quand est-ce que le marché termine aujourd'hui? (Because we want to buy things here. Please, sir, when does the market end today?)

Le gardien. Hmmm . . . bientôt! Mais, vous avez l'intention d'acheter quoi ici? Des chevaux? Des vaches? Nous n'avons pas beaucoup de chevaux et de vaches! (Hmmm . . . soon! But, what are you planning to buy here? Horses? Cows? We don't have a lot of horses and cows!)

Thibault. **Non, non. Nous avons besoin d'acheter des fruits et des légumes, c'est tout.** (No, no. We need to buy fruit and vegetables, that's all.)

Le gardien, *turning his attention back to* ***le meunier*****. Et vous, monsieur. Pourquoi est-ce que vous portez votre âne sur la tête?** (And you, sir. Why are you carrying a donkey on your head?)

Le meunier, *who has been getting tired of so many questions, especially the last one, replies.* **Encore une question! C'est assez! Oui, je porte mon âne sur la tête. Est-ce que c'est un problème!? Et vous, pourquoi est-ce que vous ne portez pas votre chien sur la tête? Combien de questions est-ce que vous avez? Nous sommes fatigués! Nous avons faim! Nous avons envie d'entrer!** (Another question! That's enough! Yes, I'm carrying my donkey on my head. Is that a problem!? And you, why aren't you carrying your dog on your head? How many questions do you have? We're tired! We're hungry! We want to come in!)

Le gardien, *surprised*. **Bon, euh, je suis désolé. Entrez, entrez!** (Oh, um, I'm sorry. Come in, come in!)

Chapitre 6

Dialogue [06_01/Tr. 27]

The miller immediately sets off to start bargaining, leaving Jean, Aurélie, and Thibault to wander around the bustling streets of the market town. Before long, they stumble upon a strange sight.

Thibault. **Jean, Aurélie? Est-ce que vous regardez les deux rats là-bas? Qu'est-ce qu'ils font?** (Jean, Aurélie? Are you looking at the two rats over there? What are they doing?)

Jean. I have no idea . . . **mais ça a l'air bizarre** (but it seems strange)**!**

Aurélie. **Hé, ho! Les rats! Qu'est-ce que vous faites là? Qu'est-ce que vous avez?** (Hey! Rats! What are you doing there? What do you have?)

Rat #1, *quietly*. **Chut! C'est un œuf! Mais chut! Le renard arrive! Il aime manger nos œufs.** (Shh! It's an egg! But shhh! The fox is coming! He likes to eat our eggs.)

Aurélie, *whispering*. **OK, mais pourquoi est-ce que tu es sur ton dos avec l'œuf dans les pattes?** (OK, but why are you on your back with the egg in your paws?)

Jean, *to the other rat*. **Oui! Et, pourquoi est-ce que tu tires ton ami par la queue?** (Yes! And, why are you pulling your friend by the tail?)

Rat #1, *in a hushed voice*. **Chuuuuut! Nous n'avons pas envie de casser notre œuf . . .** (Shhhhhhh! We don't want to break our egg . . .)

Rat #2. **Mais nous avons besoin de cacher notre œuf parce que le renard arrive.** (But we need to hide our egg because the fox is coming.)

THIBAULT, *speaking normally.* **C'est *votre* œuf?** (It's *your* egg?)

RAT #2. **CHUUUT! S'IL VOUS PLAÎT!! . . . Mais oui! Les gentilles dames ici au marché laissent toujours des œufs pour nous . . .** (SHHHH! PLEASE!! . . . Of course! The nice ladies here in the market always leave eggs for us . . .)

JEAN. Hmm . . . I've heard that kind of story before . . .

RAT #1. **C'est vrai! Elles font toujours ça, les vieilles dames du marché.** (It's true! They always do that, the old ladies from the market.)

THIBAULT. **C'est bizarre, votre manière de porter un œuf.** (It's strange, your way of carrying an egg.) But I guess so is *eating* raw egg . . .

RAT #2, *forgetting his fear, his pride now wounded.* **Ah mais, nous ne mangeons pas les œufs comme ça! Nous faisons des omelettes.** (Oh, but we don't eat eggs like that! We make omelets.)

RAT #1. **Oh là là, nous faisons des omelettes délicieuses.** (Oh my, we make delicious omelets.)

RAT #2. **Et mon ami fait des gâteaux supers!** (And my friend makes amazing cakes!)

RAT #1. **Ça va, ça va, ils ne sont pas si bons . . .** (Oh, they're not that good . . .)

RAT #2, *turning to his friend.* **Tu fais des gâteaux magnifiques!** (You make magnificent cakes!)

RAT #1. **Ah, ben, merci . . . c'est gentil.** (Oh, well, thanks . . . that's nice.)

RAT #2. **Non, mais vraiment, je trouve tes gâteaux très, très bien. Quand tu fais le gâteau au vieux fromage—OH! Ça, j'aime beaucoup. Ah, et ton gâteau aux têtes de poissons—super!** (No, but really, I think your cakes are really, really good. When you make the cake with old cheese—OH! I like that one a lot. Oh, and your fish head cake—amazing!)

AURÉLIE, JEAN, AND THIBAULT, *under their breath.* **Dégoûtant!** (Disgusting!)

Chapitre 7

Dialogue [07_01/Tr. 33]

THIBAULT. **Alors, je veux aller à la ville avec vous, mais je dois parler avec mon père.** (So, I want to go to the city with you, but I have to speak with my father.) If he thinks it's all right, then we can leave right from here—this gate leads right out to the city.

AURÉLIE. **Est-ce qu'il est près d'ici, ton père?** (Is your father near here?)

THIBAULT, *pointing at the stand of one of last merchants before the gate.* **Oui! Il est là-bas.** (Yes! He's over there.) I think he's trying to trade our donkey. *They approach from behind and begin to pick up snippets of the conversation.*

Le meunier. . . . un sac de pommes, cinq sacs de fraises, cinq sacs de pêches, et trois bons fromages? (. . . a bag of apples, five bags of strawberries, five bags of peaches, and three good cheeses?)

La dame. Non monsieur! Je ne peux pas! C'est trop. (No, sir! I can't! It's too much.)

Le meunier, *getting frustrated.* **Alors, je veux un sac de pommes, un de pommes de terre, un de tomates et trois fromages . . . ça, ça va?** (So, I want a bag of apples, one of potatoes, one of tomatoes and three cheeses . . . does that work?)

La dame. **Ben non, monsieur**. (No, sir.)

Le meunier. S'il vous plaît! (Please!)

La dame. **Vous ne pouvez pas avoir les fruits, les légumes, *et* le fromage tout pour votre petit âne . . .** (You can't have fruit, vegetables, *and* cheese all for your little donkey . . .) This cheese costs more than your donkey alone! **Il est de la ville, mon fromage. C'est très cher!** (My cheese is from the city. It's very expensive!)

Le meunier. And you think my donkey isn't expensive? Just look at him! **Regarde sa tête! Regarde ses pattes! Sa queue! Son dos!** (Look at his head! Look at his feet! His tail! His back!) He's worth a fortune!

Thibault, *interrupting.* **Papa, Aurélie et Jean veulent aller à la ville maintenant. Est-ce que nous pouvons aller ensemble?** (Papa, Aurélie and Jean want to go to the city now. Can we go together?)

Le meunier. Hmmm . . . vous voulez aller ensemble? Je ne suis pas sûr . . . la ville est loin. Ben . . . (Hmmm . . . you want to go together? I'm not sure . . . the city is far. Well . . .), *seeing the woman scowling at him from behind her cheeses.* If you can bring back **trois bons fromages de la ville . . . oui, tu peux aller avec Jean et Aurélie** (three good cheeses from the city . . . yes, you can go with Jean and Aurelie). You'd make your mother quite happy, too, seeing as I won't be bringing any home . . . **puisque le fromage ici est si cher . . .** (since the cheese here is so expensive . . .), *he scowls back at the woman.*

Thibault. **Génial! Merci, Papa!** (Great! Thanks, Papa!)

Jean and Aurélie. **Merci, monsieur!** (Thanks, sir!)

Jean. **Nous pouvons trouver les fromages, pas de problème. Allons-y!** (We can find cheese, no problem. Let's go!)

Chapitre 8

Dialogue [08_01/Tr. 39]

Striking out on the road again, the travelers swap stories about zoo life and village life, the city and the country, people and animals alike. The long, flat road takes a straight course to the city, and eventually the fields begin to give way to more and more trees. It is under one of these that the travelers meet our next curious—but probably familiar—character.

Le lapin (The Rabbit). **Excusez-moi, les amis. Quelle heure est-il?** (Excuse me, friends. What time is it?)

Thibault. **Bonjour petit lapin! Il est onze heures. Mais qu'est-ce que tu fais là?** (Hello, little rabbit! It's eleven o'clock. But what are you doing there?)

Le lapin. Pas grand-chose. (Not much.) Just relaxing, catching a few winks. You should try it. **Vous marchez trop vite! D'où est-ce que vous venez?** (You're walking too fast! Where are you coming from?)

Thibault. **Nous venons du village. Et toi?** (We're coming from the village. And you?)

Le lapin. Je viens aussi du village! J'attends mon amie, la tortue. Elle arrive, je suis sûr. Nous faisons une course à pied. (I'm coming from the village, too! I'm waiting for my friend, the Turtle. She's coming, I'm sure. We're racing.)

Aurélie. **Vous faites une course à pied . . . et tu dors?** (You're racing . . . and you're sleeping?)

Le lapin. Bien sûr, je dors! Il est onze heures! (Of course, I'm sleeping! It's eleven o'clock!) It's still early! How am I supposed to run so fast without a few *zzzzs* every so often?

Aurélie. **Tu dois courir! Pourquoi est-ce que tu attends ton amie?** (You should run! Why are you waiting for your friend?)

Le lapin. Oh, je n'ai pas peur de mon amie, la tortue. Je cours très vite. Mais les tortues? Elles sont très lentes! (Oh, I'm not afraid of my friend, the Turtle. I run very fast. But turtles? They're very slow!)

Jean. **Aurélie, il a raison.** (Aurélie, he's right.) Turtles are pretty slow. But I'm sure that you will be on your way soon, right?

Le lapin. Ben, non. (Well, no.) After my nap I was going to pick some fruit around here. **Les arbres ici sont magnifiques, n'est-ce pas? C'est délicieux, toutes les poires, les cerises! Alors, aujourd'hui, je dors et je mange.** (The trees here are amazing, aren't they? The pears and cherries are delicious! So, today, I'm sleeping and I'm eating.) Maybe I'll run tomorrow.

Aurélie. **Mais tu es fou!** (You're crazy!)

Thibault, *also dumbfounded.* **Bon, ben . . . bonne chance.** (Well, then . . . good luck.) We need to be continuing on!

Le lapin. Au revoir! (Good-bye!)

Jean. **Bon appétit!** (Enjoy your meal!)

Chapitre 9

Dialogue [09_01/Tr. 45]

The travelers' path dips and bends through stretches of orchards and gardens with small houses set back from the road. Before long, they can't resist the temptation to stray from the road and explore the fruit trees and vines.

Thibault. **Ouah, nous n'avons pas de fruit comme ça chez moi.** (Wow, we don't have fruit like that where I come from.)

Jean. **Nous non plus. Est-ce que vous voyez tous les pommiers et les cerisiers?!** (Us neither.[1] Do you see those apple trees and cherry trees?!)

Aurélie. **Et les vignes avec tous les raisins! Ils ont l'air délicieux!** (And the vines with all the grapes! They look delicious!)

Le renard boudeur (The Mopey Fox), *surprising the three friends from behind.* **Oh, vous allez manger les raisins?** (You're going to eat the grapes?)

Aurélie. **Ouah! Encore un renard!** (Wow! Another fox!)

Thibault. **Bonjour, mon ami. Oui, oui. Nous allons manger les raisins—pourquoi?** (Hello, my friend. Yes, yes. We're going to eat the grapes—why?) They don't belong to you, do they? They're just growing wild here, it seems.

Le renard boudeur. Non, non, ce ne sont pas mes raisins. Mais ce n'est pas une bonne idée. Vous n'allez pas aimer les raisins. (No, no, they aren't my grapes. But it's not a good idea. You're not going to like those grapes.)

Jean. **Ah, est-ce que les raisins ne sont pas bons?** (Oh, the grapes aren't good?)

Le renard boudeur. Non. (No.)

Thibault. **D'accord, je comprends maintenant. Est-ce que tu viens d'ici?** (OK, I understand now. Are you from around here?)

Le renard boudeur. Non. (No.)

Thibault. **Mais tu manges souvent les raisins ici, alors?** (But you eat the grapes here often, then?)

Le renard boudeur. Non. (No.)

Thibault. **Euh . . . alors, je ne comprends pas. Comment est-ce que tu sais que les raisins sont mauvais?** (Um . . . then, I don't understand. How do you know the grapes are bad?) Have you ever tried them?

Le renard boudeur. Je ne peux pas. (I can't.) They're too high for me to pick them.

1. A more standard way to say this in English would be, "We don't either" or "Neither do we."

THIBAULT. You mean you can't reach the grapes, **mais tu sais qu'ils sont mauvais** (but you know they're bad)?

LE RENARD BOUDEUR. Si je ne peux pas manger les raisins, ils ne peuvent pas être très bons. (If I can't eat the grapes, they can't be very good.) I'm just warning you. **Mais j'ai faim. Je vais chercher les œufs de la ferme... vous pouvez manger les raisins si vous voulez. Moi, je pars.** (But I'm hungry. I'm going to go look for the eggs from the farm . . . you can eat the grapes if you want. Me, I'm leaving.)

JEAN, *as* ***Le renard boudeur*** *shuffles away.* That fox had some strange ideas about grapes, I dare say.

THIBAULT. I agree. I'm not quite sure what to make of all this, but I bet I know what Aurélie is thinking. **Tu vas manger les raisins, n'est-ce pas?** (You're going to eat the grapes, right?)

AURÉLIE. **Bien sûr!** (Of course!)

Chapitre 11

Dialogue [11_01/Tr. 56]

Full of fresh fruit, our travelers spend a pleasant night under the stars. The distant lights of the city appear faintly on the horizon. The next morning, traffic on the road begins to pick up, and among the many wagons and carts rolling along, the three companions happen upon a rather slow-moving voyager.

AURÉLIE. **Hé oh! Je vois une tortue, là-bas. C'est peut-être l'amie du lapin!** (Hey! I see a turtle over there. Maybe it's the rabbit's friend!)

THIBAULT. **Je pense que tu as raison, Aurélie.** (I think you're right, Aurélie.) Let's go talk to her—we can at least tell her that she's winning their race by a long shot. **Elle va être contente.** (She's going to be happy.)

They catch up to the tortoise.

JEAN. **Bonjour, mademoiselle la tortue!** (Hello, Miss Turtle!)

MADEMOISELLE LA TORTUE. Bonjour, bonjour! Comment allez-vous? (Hello, hello! How are you?)

JEAN. **Ben, très bien, merci.** (Well, fine, thank you.)

AURÉLIE. **Est-ce que tu es l'amie du petit lapin du village?** (Are you the friend of the little rabbit from the village?)

MLLE LA TORTUE. Ah! Vous connaissez Monsieur le lapin!? Oui, bien sûr, je suis une de ses amis. Nous faisons une course cette semaine. Nous avons commencé dimanche. (Oh!

You know Mr. Rabbit!? Yes, of course, I'm one of his friends. We are doing a race this week. We started Sunday.)

Jean. **Oui, oui, nous savons. Nous avons vu ton ami le lapin.** (Yes, yes, we know. We saw your friend the rabbit.) He was a few miles back. **Il dort, il mange—mais il ne court pas beaucoup.** (He's eating, he's sleeping—but he isn't running very much.)

Mlle la tortue. Ah bon? Ça c'est intéressant! *Très* intéressant! (Really? That's interesting! *Very* interesting!)

Jean. **Je pense que tu vas gagner, mademoiselle!** (I think you're going to win, young lady!)

Mlle la tortue. Hmmm . . . tu as raison, peut-être. (Hmmm . . . you might be right.) Even if he runs his fastest, I don't think he can catch me now. **Quand est-ce que vous avez parlé avec mon ami?** (When did you talk to my friend?)

Thibault. **Aujourd'hui, nous sommes mardi, n'est-ce pas?** (Today is Tuesday, right?)

Mlle la tortue. Oui. (Yes.)

Thibault. **Alors, nous avons vu le lapin hier, lundi. Oui, hier après-midi.** (So, we saw the rabbit yesterday, Monday. Yes, yesterday afternoon.) About seven miles behind.

Mlle la tortue. Ah bon!? Alors, il ne va pas arriver à la ville avant le soir. (Really!? Then he won't get to the city before evening.)

Aurélie. **Mais peut-être qu'il a fini de dormir! Peut-être qu'il a fini de manger! Peut-être qu'il va arriver demain matin . . . attention!** (But maybe he finished sleeping! Maybe he's done eating! Maybe he'll get there tomorrow morning . . . be careful!)

Mlle la tortue. Attention? Pourquoi est-ce que je dois faire attention? Je n'ai pas peur! Il va arriver trop tard. (Careful? Why should I be careful? I'm not afraid! He's going to arrive too late.)

Aurélie. **Ah bon? Trop tard? Comment?** (Really? Too late? What?)

Mlle la tortue. Vous marchez aussi vers la ville, n'est-ce pas? (You're walking to the city, too, right?)

Jean. **Oui, et alors?** (Yes, so?)

Mlle la tortue. Eh ben, nous allons arriver ce soir! (Well, we are going to arrive tonight!)

Chapitre 12

Dialogue [12_01/Tr. 62]

The road is getting busier with each passing hour, so the four travelers shift toward the shoulder of the road. ***Mademoiselle la Tortue*** *peppers Jean, Aurélie, and Thibault with questions about their trip to the city . . .*

Mlle la Tortue. So, exactly how far have you all come? Are you just on your way up from the orchards?

Jean. **Pas du tout! Nous avons commencé dans la forêt. Nous avons marché de la forêt aux montagnes. Ensuite, nous avons marché des montagnes au fleuve. Du fleuve, nous sommes entrés au village.** (Not at all! We started in the forest. We walked from the forest to the mountains. Then, we walked from the mountains to the river. From the river, we went into the village.)

Thibault. That's when I first saw them. **J'ai rencontré Aurélie et Jean dans le village.** (I met Aurélie and Jean in the village.)

Aurélie. **Et finalement, nous sommes partis pour la ville.** (And finally, we left for the city.)

Mlle la Tortue. Ouah! Incroyable! Vous avez fait un grand voyage! Vous marchez très, très vite! (Wow! Incredible! You've had a long journey! You walk very, very fast!)

Jean. **Oui, et nous n'avons pas fini. Nous retournons chez nous—au zoo.** (Yes, and we haven't finished. We're going back to our home—in the zoo.)

Mlle la Tortue, *turning to Thibault.* You . . . you don't look like you live in the zoo.

Thibault. **Oui, tu as raison. J'habite dans mon village. Mais je ne suis jamais parti du village, alors j'ai voulu voir la ville.** (Yes, you're right. I live in my village. But I've never left the village, so I wanted to see the city.) When Aurélie and Jean told me about their plans to go back, **j'ai eu envie de venir** (I wanted to come)!

Mlle la Tortue. Ah! Tu n'as jamais vu la ville? Tu vas beaucoup aimer la ville. C'est chouette! (Oh! You've never seen the city? You're really going to like the city. It's cool!)

Thibault. **Tout le monde dit ça!** (Everyone says that!)

Mlle la Tortue. Qu'est-ce que vous allez faire là-bas? Seulement visiter le zoo? (What are you going to do there? Just visit the zoo?)

Thibault. Well, aside from Aurélie and Jean getting back home, **nous avons une chose très importante à faire** (we have something very important to do).

Mlle la Tortue. Hmmm . . . voir les musées? (Hmmm . . . see the museums?)

THIBAULT. **Non. Nous n'allons pas voir les musées . . .** (No. We're not going to see the museums . . .)

MLLE LA TORTUE. **Aller au restaurant?** (Go to a restaurant?)

JEAN. **Non. Les vaches ne peuvent pas manger dans les restaurants.** (No. Cows can't eat in restaurants.)

AURÉLIE, *hurt*. **Et les souris!?** (And mice can!?)

MLLE LA TORTUE. **Hmmm . . . alors, faire du shopping?** (Hmmm . . . then, go shopping?)

THIBAULT. **Pas vraiment . . .** (Not really . . .)

MLLE LA TORTUE. **Ben, je ne sais pas, alors. Quoi?** (Well, I don't know then. What?)

THIBAULT. **Nous allons acheter du fromage.** (We're going to buy cheese.)

Chapitre 13

Dialogue [13_01/Tr. 68]

The travelers finally reach the city's gate and enter triumphantly.

THIBAULT. **Nous sommes arrivés! Après deux jours!** (We're here! After two days!)

MLLE LA TORTUE. **Oui, félicitations! Vous avez réussi votre voyage.** (Yes, congratulations! You finished your journey.)

AURÉLIE. **Et félicitations à toi aussi, mademoiselle la Tortue: tu as gagné la course avec ton ami le lapin. Sans courir!** (And congratulations to you, too, Miss Turtle: You've won the race with your friend the rabbit. Without running!)

MLLE LA TORTUE. **Oui, mais aussi je suis venue à la ville sans faire de pause** (Yes, but I've also come to the city without stopping)—that's what counts. **Vous voyez** (You see), I didn't really dilly-dally **comme mon ami: je ne suis pas restée sous les arbres à côté de la route comme lui, je n'ai pas mangé de fruits comme lui** (like my friend: I didn't stay under the trees beside the road like him, I didn't eat fruit like him)**.** And above all, **je n'ai jamais dormi au milieu de l'après-midi comme lui** (I never slept in the middle of the afternoon like him)!

JEAN. **Très bien!** (Very good!) So. Where to now, **mes amis** (my friends)?

MLLE LA TORTUE. **Moi, je vais attendre mon ami ici, donc, je pense que je vais dire "au revoir" maintenant. J'ai été contente de marcher avec vous!** (I'm going to wait for my friend here, so I think I'll say good-bye now. I'm happy to have walked with you!)

THIBAULT. **Nous aussi! Merci . . . et à bientôt, nous espérons.** (Us, too! Thanks . . . and see you soon, we hope.)

JEAN, AURÉLIE. **Bonne soirée!** (Have a nice evening!)

Thibault, Aurélie, and Jean wander into the city, where shops and businesses are closing down for the night.

Jean. **Hmm . . . Quelle heure est-il?** (Hmm . . . What time is it?)

Thibault. **Je ne sais pas—il est six heures, ou sept heures peut-être. Les magasins ferment.** (I don't know—it's six o'clock, or maybe seven o'clock. The stores are closing.)

Aurélie. **Mince! Nous devons aller vite, alors. Le zoo ferme à huit heures. Thibault, est-ce que nous pouvons acheter ton fromage demain?** (Oh no! We should go quickly, then. The zoo closes at eight o'clock. Thibault, can we buy your cheese tomorrow?)

Thibault. **Pas de problème.** (No problem.)

Jean. **Et est-ce que ça va pour toi de dormir avec tous les animaux?** (And is it OK with you to sleep with all the animals?)

Thibault. **Oui, oui, je peux dormir avec eux.** (Yes, yes, I can sleep with them.) Honestly, I'm so tired I could sleep anywhere at this point!

Aurélie. **Moi aussi.** (Me, too.)

Jean. **Je suis d'accord.** (I agree.) *The three head off down the street. After a short distance, Jean pauses and whispers to Aurélie . . .* **Mais, entre nous, est-ce que tu sais pourquoi je suis vraiment content de retourner chez nous?** (But, between us, do you know why I'm really happy to get home?)

Aurélie. **Non, pourquoi?** (No, why?)

Jean. **Parce que finalement, après notre grand voyage, nous allons être avec des animaux normaux!** (Because finally, after our long journey, we'll be with animals that are normal!)

Chapitre 14

Dialogue [14_01/Tr. 75]

Jean, Aurélie, and Thibault are searching for a place in the zoo to sleep for the night.

Jean. **Alors, Aurélie, où est-ce que nous dormons ce soir?** (So, Aurélie, where are we sleeping tonight?)

Aurélie. **Je vais me coucher avec mes amies, les vaches. Elles se trouvent pas loin d'ici. Vous pouvez venir si vous voulez!** (I am going to sleep with my friends, the cows. They are located not far from here. You can come if you want!)

Thibault. **Parfait!** (Perfect!)

Jean. **Parfait!** (Perfect!)

Thibault. I didn't plan to spend my first night in the city sleeping with cattle, but it's as good a place as any. Where can I brush my teeth?

Aurélie. **Eeeuuhhh . . . les vaches ne se brossent pas les dents.** (Ummm. . . . Cows do not brush their teeth.)

Thibault. **Ah bon? Ben . . . d'accord.** (Oh really? Well . . . OK.) Where can I wash up, then?

Aurélie. **Eeeuuhh, désolée. Les vaches ne se lavent pas non plus.** (Ummm . . . sorry. Cows do not wash up either.)

Thibault. **Ça alors!** (Well then!)

Jean. Well, that simplifies things, I guess. **À quelle heure est-ce que nous nous levons demain?** (What time are we waking up tomorrow?)

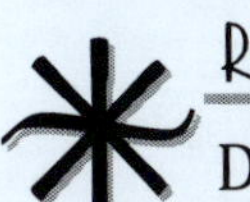

Renvoi

Do you remember how to tell time in French? If not, take a look back at **chapitre** 8 to refresh your memory.

Thibault. Not terribly early, I say. I won't need time to wash up or brush my teeth, after all. Ahem! *Thibault looks jokingly at Aurélie.* **Je pense que ça va si nous nous levons à neuf heures. Nous nous couchons tôt ce soir, donc ça ne doit pas être un problème.** (I think it is fine if we wake up at nine o'clock. We are going to bed early this evening, so it should not be a problem.)

Jean. **Parfait! Comme ça, nous allons avoir le temps d'acheter tes fromages, Thibault. Ensuite, nous pouvons nous promener dans la ville ensemble.** (Perfect! That way, we will have the time to buy your cheeses, Thibault. Then, we can go for a walk in the city together.) We'll see lots of beautiful sights.

Thibault. **Génial! Mais d'abord, j'ai *très* faim—est-ce qu'il y a quelque chose à manger dans le zoo?** (Great! But first, I am very hungry. Is there something to eat in the zoo?)

Jean. **Mmm . . . j'ai eu la même idée, Thibault! Je veux manger avant de me coucher!** (Mmm . . . I had the same idea, Thibault! I want to eat before going to bed!)

Aurélie. **Eh ben, vous devez venir avec moi pour rencontrer les vaches! Nous ne nous brossons pas les dents, et nous ne nous lavons pas, mais *manger*! ça, nous savons faire.** (Well, you should come with me to meet the cows! We don't brush our teeth, and we don't wash up, but *eat*! that we know how to do.)

Chapter 15

Dialogue [15_01/Tr. 81]

Following a good meal and a solid night's sleep, the three companions slip out of the zoo to see the city. After a full day of sightseeing, delicacy tasting, and memory making, Aurélie expresses concern.

Aurélie. **Allons-y les amis! Nous devons nous dépêcher si nous voulons acheter les fromages. Il est déjà huit heures!** (Let's go, friends! We should hurry if we want to buy the cheeses. It is already eight o'clock!)

Jean. **Mince! Aurélie a raison!** (Shoot! Aurélie is right.) They may have already sold out.

Thibault, *smiling*. **Pourquoi est-ce que vous vous inquiétez? Je me suis occupé de ça! J'ai appelé ce matin** (Why are you worrying? I took care of that! I called this morning)—I reserved three big wheels. As soon as I woke up, **je me suis souvenu** (I remembered)!

Aurélie. **Oh purée, il est fort, Thibault!** (Holy smokes! He's good, that Thibault!)

The three friends head to the shop to pick up Thibault's order. Upon leaving, Jean reflects.

Jean. **Tu sais, Thibault, nous ne rencontrons pas souvent des garçons comme toi au zoo. Nous allons nous souvenir de toi!** (You know, Thibault, we do not often meet boys like you at the zoo. We will remember you!)

Thibault. **Et moi, je vais me souvenir de vous. Nous nous sommes amusés ensemble!** (And I will remember you. We had fun together!)

Aurélie. **Est-ce que tu vas te souvenir de comment retourner au zoo?** (Will you remember how to return to the zoo?)

Thibault. **Bien sûr! Et je vais venir avec toute ma famille.** (Of course! And I will come with all my family.)

Jean. **Super. Je pense que Aurélie et moi, nous préférons rester dans la ville maintenant—la campagne, c'est bien, mais nous nous sentons mieux au zoo!** (Super. I think that Aurélie and I, we prefer to stay in the city now—the countryside is fine, but we feel better at the zoo!)

Thibault. **Et moi, je me sens bien à la campagne.** (And I feel better in the countryside.) But visiting friends is always worth a journey!

Jean. And so is a **bon fromage** (good cheese)!

Appendix B

Chant Translations

Chapitre 1

To Be or Not to Be [01_02/Tr. 2]

Chant (ahem, rap)	Translation
Les garçons: Je suis beau. (Yo!)	The boys: I am handsome. (Yo!)
Les filles: Je suis belle. (Belle!)	The girls: I am beautiful. (Beautiful!)
Tu es beau. (Yo!)	You are handsome. (Yo!)
Tu es belle. (Belle!)	You are beautiful. (Beautiful!)
Il est beau. (Yo!)	He is handsome. (Yo!)
(Et elle est belle, belle, belle, belle!)	(And she is beautiful, beautiful, beautiful, beautiful!)
Nous sommes beaux. (Yo!)	We are handsome. (Yo!)
Vous êtes beaux. (Yo!)	You are handsome. (Yo!)
Vous êtes belles. (Belles!)	You are beautiful. (Beautiful!)
Ils sont beaux (Yo, yo!)	They are handsome. (Yo, yo!)
(Et elles sont belles, belles, belles, belles!)	(And they are beautiful, beautiful, beautiful, beautiful!)

Être (to be) [01_03/Tr. 3]

Person	Singular	Plural
1st Person	**je suis** (I am)	**nous sommes** (we are)
2nd Person	**tu es** (you are)	**vous êtes** (you are)
3rd Person	**il/elle est** (he/she/it is)	**ils/elles sont** (they are)

Chapitre 2

Aller (to go) [02_02/Tr. 9]

Person	Singular	Plural
1st Person	**je vais** (I go)	**nous allons** (we go)
2nd Person	**tu vas** (you go)	**vous allez** (you go)
3rd Person	**il/elle va** (he/she/it goes)	**ils/elles vont** (they go)

Chapitre 3

Je ne mange pas de fromage. (I don't eat cheese.) [03_02/Tr. 15]

A lost poem from the miller's wife from her childhood (before imported cheese) . . .

Chant	Translation
Je ne mange pas de fromage.	I do not eat cheese.
Il n'est pas bon dans mon village.	It is not good in my village.
Puisque je n'aime pas marcher loin,	Since I do not like to walk far,
Je reste ici, et mange le pain.	I stay here, and eat the bread.

Chapitre 4

Est-ce que tu chantes? (Do you sing?) [04_02/Tr. 21]

Chant	Translation
Est-ce que tu chantes? *Oui, beaucoup.*	Do you sing? *Yes, a lot.*
Et tu chantes quoi? *Je chante le blues.*	And what do you sing? *I sing the blues.*
Pourquoi est-ce que tu chantes? *Je ne suis pas content!*	Why do you sing? *I'm not happy!*
Quand est-ce que tu chantes? *Maintenant!*	When are you singing? *Now!*
Ah . . . au revoir, alors!	Ah . . . goodbye, then!

Chapitre 6

Faire (to do/make) [06_02/Tr. 28]

Person	Singular	Plural
1st Person	**je fais** (I do/I make)	**nous faisons** (we do/we make)
2nd Person	**tu fais** (you do/you make)	**vous faites** (you do/you make)
3rd Person	**il/elle fait** (he/she/it does; he/she/it makes)	**ils/elles font** (they do/they make)

Chapitre 7

Pouvoir (to be able to/can) [07_02/Tr. 34]

Person	Singular	Plural
1st Person	**je peux** (I can)	**nous pouvons** (we can)
2nd Person	**tu peux** (you can)	**vous pouvez** (you can)
3rd Person	**il/elle peut** (he/she/it can)	**ils/elles peuvent** (they can)

Chapitre 8

Il est sept heures. (It is seven o'clock.) [08_02/Tr. 40][1]

Chant	Translation
Il est sept heures, déjà, alors, il est sept heures, et toi tu dors.	It is seven o'clock, already, so, it is seven o'clock, and you, you are sleeping.
Il est huit heures, déjà, alors, il est huit heures et toi tu dors.	It is eight o'clock, already, so, it is eight o'clock and you, you are sleeping.
Il est neuf heures, déjà, alors! Il est neuf heures, et toi tu dors.	It is nine o'clock, already, so! It is nine o'clock and you, you are sleeping.
Il est dix heures, déjà! Alors! Il est dix heures, tu dors encore!	It is ten o'clock, already! So! It is ten o'clock, you are still sleeping![1]
Tout ça n'est pas très amusant: toi tu dors, et moi j'attends!	All that is not very funny: you, you're sleeping, and me, I'm waiting!

Chapitre 9

The Future Tense—Starring the Verb Manger (to eat) [09_02/Tr. 46]

Person	Singular	Plural
1st Person	**je vais manger** (I will eat)	**nous allons manger** (we will eat)
2nd Person	**tu vas manger** (you will eat)	**vous allez manger** (you will eat)
3rd Person	**il/elle va manger** (he/she/it will eat)	**ils/elles vont manger** (they will eat)

1. In **chapitre 4**, the word **encore** was translated as "again" or "another." When used with a verb (as in this chant), it can also mean "still," as in "You're *still* sleeping!" (**Tu dors encore!**) or "You're still eating!" (**Tu manges encore!**).

Chapitre 11

Le passé composé: avoir + the Past Participle [11_02/Tr. 57]

Person	Singular	Plural
1st Person	**j'ai chanté** (I sang)	**nous avons chanté** (we sang)
2nd Person	**tu as chanté** (you sang)	**vous avez chanté** (you sang)
3rd Person	**il/elle a chanté** (he/she/it sang)	**ils/elles ont chanté** (they sang)

Chapitre 12

Mini Tour de France [12_02/Tr. 63]

Chant	Translation
Paris, c'est beau, Paris—je suis retourné.	Paris, it's beautiful, Paris, I returned.
L'Alsace est belle, très belle—il est retourné.	Alsace is beautiful, very beautiful—he returned.
La Provence est superbe, ah oui, superbe—elle est retournée.	Provence is superb, ah yes, superb—she returned.
Et la Bretagne, la Normandie? Magnifique, magnifique!—ils sont retournés . . .	And Brittany? Normandy? Magnificent! Magnificent!—they returned . . .
elles sont retournées, nous sommes retournés, vous êtes retournés!	they returned, we returned, you returned!
Et toi, tu es retourné?	And you, you returned? *or* And you, did you return?

Le passé composé II: être + the past participle [12_03/Tr. 64]

Person	Singular	Plural
1st Person	**je suis retourné** (I returned)	**nous sommes retournés** (we returned)
2nd Person	**tu es retourné** (you returned)	**vous êtes retournés** (you returned)
3rd Person	**il est retourné** (he/it returned) **elle est retournée** (she/it returned)	**ils sont retournés** (they returned) **elles sont retournées** (they, f. returned)

Chapitre 13

Stressed Pronouns: Moi, je suis beau! (I'm handsome!) [13_02/Tr. 70][2]

Chant	Translation
Moi, je suis beau!	Me, I am handsome!
Moi, je suis intelligent!	Me, I am intelligent!
Moi, je suis magnifique!	Me, I am magnificent!
Moi, je suis sympathique!	Me, I am nice!
Hmmm . . . toi, tu es orgueilleux!!![2]	Hmmm . . . You, you are proud!

Person	Singular	Plural
1st Person	**moi** (me)	**nous** (we)
2nd Person	**toi** (you)	**vous** (you)
3rd Person	**lui/elle** (him/her/it)	**eux/elles** (them)

Chapitre 14

Pronominal Verbs—Je me lève (I get up) [14_02/Tr. 77]

Person	Singular	Plural
1st Person	**je me lève** (I get up)	**nous nous levons** (we get up)
2nd Person	**tu te lèves** (you get up)	**vous vous levez** (you get up)
3rd Person	**il/elle se lève** (he/she/it gets up)	**ils/elles se lèvent** (they get up)

Chapitre 15

Past-Tense Pronominals—Je me suis amusé. (I had fun.) [15_02/Tr. 83]

Person	Singular	Plural
1st Person	**je me suis amusé(e)** (I had fun)	**nous nous sommes amusé(e)s** (we had fun)
2nd Person	**tu t'es amusé(e)** (you had fun)	**vous vous êtes amusé(e)(s)** (you had fun)
3rd Person	**il s'est amusé/elle s'est amusée** (he had fun/she had fun)	**ils se sont amusés/elles se sont amusées** (they had fun)

2. **Orgueilleux** means "proud" or "self-centered" in English.

Appendix C

Verbs

Regular Verbs

-er Verbs

(All **-er** verbs will have the same conjugation pattern as **parler**.)

Parler *(to speak/talk)* *(*FFCA chapitre *1)*

Person	Singular	Plural
1st Person	**je parle** (I speak/talk)	**nous parlons** (we speak/talk)
2nd Person	**tu parles** (you speak/talk)	**vous parlez** (you [all] speak/talk)
3rd Person	**il/elle parle** (he/she/it speaks/talks)	**ils/elles parlent** (they, masculine/they, feminine speak/talk)
p.p. **parlé**		

-ir Verbs

(All *regular*[1] **-ir** verbs will have the same conjugation pattern as **finir**.)

Finir *(to finish)* *(*FFCA chapitre *3)*

Person	Singular	Plural
1st Person	**je finis** (I finish)	**nous finissons** (we finish)
2nd Person	**tu finis** (you finish)	**vous finissez** (you all finish)
3rd Person	**il/elle finit** (he/she/it finishes)	**ils/elles finissent** (they finish)
p.p. **fini**		

1. Some **-ir** verbs are irregular, such as **dormir**, which is also in this appendix.

Irregular Verbs

Attendre *(to wait)* (FFCB chapitre *8)*

Person	Singular	Plural
1st Person	**j'attends** (I wait)	**nous attendons** (we wait)
2nd Person	**tu attends** (you wait)	**vous attendez** (you wait)
3rd Person	**il/elle attend** (he/she/it waits)	**ils/elles attendent** (they wait)
p.p. **attendu**		

Avoir *(to have)* (FFCA chapitre *8)*

Person	Singular	Plural
1st Person	**j'ai** (I have)	**nous avons** (we have)
2nd Person	**tu as** (you have)	**vous avez** (you have)
3rd Person	**il/elle a** (he/she/it has)	**ils/elles ont** (they have)
p.p. **eu**		

Courir *(to run)* (FFCB chapitre *8)*

Person	Singular	Plural
1st Person	**je cours** (I run)	**nous courons** (we run)
2nd Person	**tu cours** (you run)	**vous courez** (you run)
3rd Person	**il/elle court** (he/she/it runs)	**ils/elles courent** (they run)
p.p. **couru**		

Connaître *(to know)* (FFCB chapitre *11)*

Person	Singular	Plural
1st Person	**je connais** (I know)	**nous connaissons** (we know)
2nd Person	**tu connais** (you know)	**vous connaissez** (you know)
3rd Person	**il/elle connaît** (he/she/it knows)	**ils/elles connaissent** (they know)
p.p. **connu**		

Dormir *(to sleep)* (FFCB chapitre *8)*

*Note that the conjugation of **s'endormir** (to fall asleep) is based on **dormir**—just add **en**!*

Person	Singular	Plural
1st Person	**je dors** (I sleep)	**nous dormons** (we sleep)
2nd Person	**tu dors** (you sleep)	**vous dormez** (you sleep)
3rd Person	**il/elle dort** (he/she/it sleeps)	**ils/elles dorment** (they sleep)
p.p. **dormi**		

Être *(to be)* (FFCB chapitre *1)*

Person	Singular	Plural
1st Person	**je suis** (I am)	**nous sommes** (we are)
2nd Person	**tu es** (you are)	**vous êtes** (you are)
3rd Person	**il/elle est** (he/she/it is)	**ils/elles sont** (they are)
p.p. **été**		

Faire *(to do/make)* (FFCB chapitre *6)*

Person	Singular	Plural
1st Person	**je fais** (I do/make)	**nous faisons** (we do/make)
2nd Person	**tu fais** (you do/make)	**vous faites** (you do/make)
3rd Person	**il/elle fait** (he/she/it does/makes)	**ils/elles font** (they do/make)
p.p. **fait**		

Partir *(to leave)* (FFCB chapitre *9)*

Person	Singular	Plural
1st Person	**je pars** (I leave)	**nous partons** (we leave)
2nd Person	**tu pars** (you leave)	**vous partez** (you leave)
3rd Person	**il/elle part** (he/she/it leaves)	**ils/elles partent** (they leave)
p.p. **parti**		

Pouvoir *(to be able to/can)* (FFCB chapitre *7)*

Person	Singular	Plural
1st Person	**je peux** (I can)	**nous pouvons** (we can)
2nd Person	**tu peux** (you can)	**vous pouvez** (you can)
3rd Person	**il/elle peut** (he/she/it can)	**ils/elles peuvent** (they can)
p.p. **pu**		

Prendre *(to take)* (FFCB chapitre *9)*

Person	Singular	Plural
1st Person	**je prends** (I take)	**nous prenons** (we take)
2nd Person	**tu prends** (you take)	**vous prenez** (you take)
3rd Person	**il/elle prend** (he/she/it takes)	**ils/elles prennent** (they take)
p.p. **pris**		

Savoir *(to know)* *(FFCB chapitre 9)*

Person	Singular	Plural
1st Person	**je sais** (I know)	**nous savons** (we know)
2nd Person	**tu sais** (you know)	**vous savez** (you know)
3rd Person	**il/elle sait** (he/she/it knows)	**ils/elles savent** (they know)
p.p. **su**		

Venir *(to come)* *(FFCB chapitre 8)*

Note that the conjugation of ***se souvenir*** *(to remember) is based on* ***venir****—just add* ***sou****.*

Person	Singular	Plural
1st Person	**je viens** (I come)	**nous venons** (we come)
2nd Person	**tu viens** (you come)	**vous venez** (you come)
3rd Person	**il/elle vient** (he/she/it comes)	**ils/elles viennent** (they come)
p.p. **venu**		

Voir *(to see)* *(FFCB chapitre 9)*

Person	Singular	Plural
1st Person	**je vois** (I see)	**nous voyons** (we see)
2nd Person	**tu vois** (you see)	**vous voyez** (you see)
3rd Person	**il/elle voit** (he/she/it sees)	**ils/elles voient** (they see)
p.p. **vu**		

Devoir *(to have to, should)* *(FFCB chapitre 7)*

Person	Singular	Plural
1st Person	**je dois** (I have to)	**nous devons** (we have to)
2nd Person	**tu dois** (you have to)	**vous devez** (you have to)
3rd Person	**il/elle doit** (he/she/it has to)	**ils/elles doivent** (they have to)
p.p. **dû**		

Vouloir *(to want)* *(FFCB chapitre 7)*

Person	Singular	Plural
1st Person	**je veux** (I want)	**nous voulons** (we want)
2nd Person	**tu veux** (you want)	**vous voulez** (you want)
3rd Person	**il/elle veut** (he/she/it wants)	**ils/elles veulent** (they want)
p.p. **voulu**		

Dire *(to say)* (FFCB chapitre *12)*

Person	Singular	Plural
1st Person	**je dis** (I say)	**nous disons** (we say)
2nd Person	**tu dis** (you say)	**vous dites** (you say)
3rd Person	**il/elle dit** (he/she says)	**ils/elles disent** (they say)
p.p. **dit**		

S'inquiéter *(to worry)* (FFCB chapitre *15)*

Person	Singular	Plural
1st Person	**je m'inquiète** (I worry)	**nous nous inquiétons** (we worry)
2nd Person	**tu t'inquiètes** (you worry)	**vous vous inquiétez** (you worry)
3rd Person	**il/elle s'inquiète** (he/she/it worries)	**ils/elles s'inquiètent** (they worry)
p.p. **inquiété**		

Appendix D

Past Participles

Infinitive	Past Participle
parler[1]	parlé
finir[2]	fini
attendre	attendu
avoir	eu
courir	couru
connaître	connu
dormir	dormi
être	été
faire	fait
partir	parti
pouvoir	pu
prendre	pris
savoir	su
venir	venu
voir	vu
devoir	dû
vouloir	voulu
dire	dit
s'endormir	endormi
se souvenir	souvenu
s'inquiéter	inquiété

1. The past participle of all **-er** verbs will end in **-é**.
2. The past participle of all **-ir** verbs will end in **-i**.

Appendix E

Prepositions

Français (French)	**Anglais** (English)	Book/**Chapitre**
à	to, at	A/1
à côté de	next to	A/6
après	after	B/12
avant	before	B/11
avec	with	A/1
dans	in	A/4
de	of, from	A/2
derrière	behind	A/7
devant	in front of	A/6
loin (de)	far (from)	A/7
pour	for	A/2
près (de)	near (to), close (to)	A/11
sans	without	B/13
sous	under	B/13
sur	on, on top of	A/7
vers	toward	A/4

Notes

Notes

Notes